Green Greenwich

Our treasured open spaces

Candy Blackham

III Clink Street

Published by Clink Street Publishing 2025

ISBN: 978-1-915785-41-1 (paperback)
ISBN: 978-1-915785-42-8 (ebook)

Also by Candy Blackham, *Green Lewisham*

CONTENTS

FOREWORD

Greenwich could have no better or inspiring guide to its wonderful and varied green spaces than Candy Blackham's book. Its scope is breathtaking: ancient parks and commons, heathland, municipal parks, allotments, pocket parks and gardens of all kinds. She has visited, researched and photographed all of these precious green spaces in the borough. Her knowledge of plants and trees, her skill as a photographer and her sheer determination as a researcher have created a remarkable record of the borough's open spaces. I particularly like her delightful 'hymn of praise' to the less well known Bostall Community Gardens. A record of some 145 sites and walks.

The diverse and very precious areas of green space in the royal borough include many that were saved as a result of extremely hard-fought campaigns. John De Morgan and the Plumstead Rioters saved the areas of ancient common at Plumstead, one of which has an impressive bronze Age barrow. The wonderful woodlands on Shooters Hill would have succumbed to housing development without the intervention of the London County Council between the wars. However, all but one of a Bronze Age barrow cemetery on the hill was lost. A later threat from the proposed East London River Crossing and its dual carriageway through Oxleas and Shepherdleas Woods was fought off by tough, inspired community pressure and activism. The integrity of ancient Blackheath was being undermined in the nineteenth century by development pressures, gravel extraction and unregulated activities, but the takeover by the Metropolitan Board of Works preserved that large area of heathland for public enjoyment. There were even two significant threats to Greenwich Park: a railway viaduct in 1835 was designed to take the London and Greenwich Railway to Woolwich and beyond, the other a motorway tunnel planned by the Greater London Council as part of the notorious 'Motorway Box' proposals for London. Both of course failed.

Candy Blackham's thorough research, fieldwork, her knowledge of trees and plants, informed opinions and her skill with the camera make this a unique and important record of Greenwich's wonderful green spaces, providing strong evidence against any future threats.

Julian Watson

Local History Librarian for the London Borough of Greenwich,

1969–2003

INTRODUCTION

"Though the gray hair is on my head, and the furrows of time are on my brow, yet have I to be thankful for a light foot, a ready hand, a quick eye, and a cheerful heart; and the possession of these blessings, naturally enough, leads me to partake of sunshine, rather than to go in quest of shadows."
George Mogridge, *Old Humphrey's Walks in London*, (1851, The Religious Tract Society, London)

Green Lewisham was published in July 2022, but I had caught the exploring bug. And so I set off immediately to investigate the green spaces in the Royal Borough of Greenwich (RBG), armed with a new camera and new shoes!

I soon learned that exploring in this neighbouring borough would be a different experience from Lewisham. There were fewer contemporary historical books, no John Coulter as in Lewisham, and fewer dedicated bloggers to help me. Many hours of reading and research were needed. My library grew rapidly, helped by Amazon, ABE Books and others, and mostly delivered by Odile – THANK YOU ODILE! The West Greenwich Library was marvellous and the Greenwich Archive helped as and when it could.

A back injury continued to be problematic, but walking in the various green spaces always improved my mood and helped keep me fit-ish. The trees were particularly healing. The RBG is blessed with wonderful woodlands, young and old, though while we enjoy them, we also have to be mindful of how we care for them.

I became increasingly aware of the need to protect our environment and the hugely important role played by the Friends groups, and by individual people who continue to fight for the future of our natural surroundings.

And I found that very simple things could make all the difference — information boards, requests for care, dead hedging, controlling children and dogs in planted areas. And with that awareness was also a sadness that some people can be so careless, allowing children to break branches and pick flowers in parks, thereby teaching them that it doesn't matter what they do to public property.

So, over time, this became a book both joyous and sad, and with an increasing gratitude to those people who care, go out of their way to maintain high standards, and have an empathy with nature.

I am immensely grateful to all those who keep me on my feet: Dr Sharya Beheshti and Katie Walker for expertise and kindness; Darren Higgins and Jacqui Norton–Old for refusing to give up; Prof Bruce Kidd who encouraged me to 'fight against the dying of the light'; Dr Paul Scott who advocated 'keep going'; Dr Serge Nikolic who is kind, and understands, and heals; Liona van Eck for helpfulness; Dr Melvin Lobo who sorted out Covid; the doctors and nurses at King's College Hospital; and Liza St Clair for her help at the gym. I am more than grateful.

Cllr Adel Khaireh and Rob Goring of RBG, Paul de Sayle from QWAG, and Zara Visanji of Thames21 all supported this project. Linda Durrant made wonderful maps again, and Julian Watson was generously supportive and encouraging.

Many generous and helpful people met me in parks, read text and saved me from factual errors: Kathy Aitken; Chris Allen; Tim and Edna Anderson; Christine Anthony; Dr Phil Askew; Christine Bevan; Mark Barnes; Tim Barnes KC; Keith Billinghurst; Sacha Bright; Shirley Brihi; John Bunney; Stella Butler; Richard Butt; Mark Cannon; Sarah Carlin; Irma Carter; John Clark; Tony Day; Meryl Davies; Jonathan Drakes; Jane Errington; Sarah Foord–Divers; Will Foster; David Jarvis; Jack Gower; Diane Greenwood; Fiona Harrison; Allen Hervey; Simon Hawkins; Rachel Henry; Carol Howcroft; Bridget Imeson; Kris Inglis; David Jarvis; Christine Johnson; Carol Kenna; John Kennett; Jim Kinsella; Dr Benz Kotzen; Kate MacLachlan; Jean Mahy; John Martin; Sarah McMichael; Kirsty Meekings; Matthew Mees; John Martin; Matilda Martinetti; Mark Maxwell; Susan Miles; Kay Millburn; Dr Mary Mills; Sue Mitchell; Linda Monks; Revd Liz Newman; Rick Newman; Anne Novis; Stephen O'Connor; Kate Parker; Terry Powley; John Reed; Barbara Reid; Revd Caroline Risden; Morgan Roberts; Jason Sylvan; John Slusar; Alan Smith; Major Scott Sloan; David Stanley; Dave Stevenson; Gulle Stubbs; Christine Thornton; Zoe Toone; Ellie Truscott; Bee Twidale; Dr Pieter van der Merwe;

Christine Wagg; Tracy Ward; Dr Tom Wareham; Pauline Watson; John Webb; Chris Whitefield; Elizabeth Wiggans; Lizzie Wood; Liz Wright; Isabel Yeardley. English Heritage and the Royal Parks were helpful, and I owe a big thank you to all the people who agreed to be photographed.

As before, the Authoright team guided me through the whole process.

Personal friends have been wonderful. My thanks to Dennis Atwell for trying out pubs and Andrina Gibson for taking delivery of books in my absence; BER for continuing and unwavering friendship; Marion Blair, Charo Gonzalez, Chrissie Kitchen, Sarah McLeery and Juliette Weaver for just being there; Fiona Harrison for introducing me to Mara Café and helpful chats over cups of coffee; Jane O'Brien for listening; Elliott Levy for urging me to 'take ownership' and be personal; Sasho Somov for his music; Ian Stockwell for caring; and finally thanks to Jeremy who walked yet more miles while listening to further 'park talk'.

The Borough of Greenwich is full of surprising sights, and I am grateful that I stepped off the path and walked round the corner so many times. And, the end, this book felt more like a community project to celebrate the efforts of all those who look after the borough's treasured green spaces.

Any mistakes are my own and much regretted.

A warm summer Sunday with Friends of The Tarn

WHY ARE THERE GREEN SPACES IN GREENWICH?

The Royal Borough of Greenwich is a story of the very old and the very new, of town and country, and of changing populations and behaviours. It is a story of trade, war, and business, and more recently concerns about climate change and the care of our environment. It is a slightly scary story about the rapid disappearance of the countryside and the importance of looking after the green spaces which are left. And it is always the story of people.

The Romans were here, as were the Saxons and the Danes (briefly). French and Belgian monasteries were Lords of the Manor for several hundred years before the land reverted to Crown ownership. And until the 19th century, much of the borough was in Kent.

It is the London borough with the longest river frontage on the Thames, stretching from Deptford to Erith, and it carries the long–distance Thames Path for 13 kms. Land rises from the former river marshes to an escarpment and then again to the high point of Shooters Hill. Woodlands are abundant but there are also grasslands — acid, neutral, chalk — some heathland, and still two patches of farmland.

The borough was once home to two royal palaces: Greenwich and Eltham. In Greenwich, the site of successive palaces lives on as Greenwich University (formerly the Royal Hospital and followed by the Royal Naval College), the Maritime Museum and Greenwich Park. In Eltham, only the great hall of Eltham Palace remains as part of the Courtaulds' Art Nouveau mansion, and its former parkland is now the Blackheath Golf Club and the Middle Park and Horn Park housing estates.

Away from the river, much of the area was still countryside well into the 20th century. Kidbrooke was farmed until WWII, and Chapel Farm and Coldharbour Farm in New Eltham were dairy farms until the 1940s. Their fields are now mainly housing with small parks and sports grounds.

The countryside gave way to the same forces which changed Lewisham: new railways and roads, London's expanding population, WWI and the changes in society thereafter, and an escalation of social expectations after WWII.

The major landowners did not share the philanthropic bent to be found in neighbouring Lewisham. Was it a question of timing, or perhaps because they didn't live locally? Mayow Park and Deptford Park in Lewisham, are parks which were created in the late 19th century by concerned local landowners who wanted to benefit in perpetuity the general public living in areas of dense housing. By contrast, the major landowners in Greenwich, such as the Angerstein family, John Cator and the Pattison family in Woolwich, sold their land for commercial development. Only the Maryon–Wilson family, who owned the Manor of Charlton, gave or sold land for public parks.

Fortunately the Councils — the GLC, the London City Council, and the Woolwich Council — saw the need for recreational spaces. Ebenezer Howard had published *Tomorrow: A Peaceful Path to Real Reform* in 1898 and started the Garden City movement. His vision was fresh in the minds of those who planned the remarkable Progress Estate in 1915. Middle Park Estate, Horn Park Estate and the Coldharbour Estate were laid out with similar ideas.

Some recent commercial housing developments seem less interested in natural and biodiverse surroundings. Royal Arsenal Riverside is very attractive but continuing development will remove a park, and by removing any responsibility for gardening from the residents, are the developers perhaps also removing a sense of ownership and responsibility for the environment? 'New London' on the north of the Greenwich Peninsula may be architecturally interesting, but does it include adequate recreational green spaces for up to 17,000 new residents?

Yet there is another way. A stark contrast is offered at Thamesmead with Peabody's commitment to 'Living in the Landscape' and placemaking; Waterford Place in New Eltham is built around a village green with a large pond;

and Kidbrooke Village is very beautiful, with parks and gardens at all levels.

Why include churchyards and cemeteries? In the 1800s, George Alfred Walker, a doctor in East London, linked poor public health to overcrowded burial grounds in densely inhabited parts of London. He argued passionately for the need to "remove as far as possible from the living, the pestiferous exhalations of the dead."[1] The Burials Act of 1852 started the process of closing overcrowded burial grounds, but what then? Further legislation — Open Spaces Acts and Disused Burial Grounds Acts — allowed these spaces to develop into public parks.

The Metropolitan Public Gardens Association was founded in 1882 by Lord Brabazon with the support of the National Health Society. The Association's remit was to acquire and lay out recreational spaces, including these newly available churchyards. The churchyards at St Alfege's in Greenwich and St Mary in Woolwich were two of their earliest gardens.

Greenwich is particularly rich in woodlands. Shooters Hill Woods, Shrewsbury Park, Bostall Woods and Bostall Heath all offer many hours of calming surroundings, but surely the undergrowth of wildflowers and bulbs must be protected from dogs and feet by deadhedging and designated paths or the joy of seeing bluebells in the spring will simply disappear.

In 1977 the London boroughs of Greenwich, Lewisham, Bexley and Bromley collaborated to create the Green Chain Walk, linking 300 open spaces to protect them from building. The fifty–three–mile walk from the Thames to Crystal Palace has several offshoots and circular routes. The TFL website suggests eleven sections, covering 82 kms.

People care deeply about their surroundings. John de Morgan was imprisoned to protect Plumstead Common from development in the 19th century, and in the 20th century campaigners blocked the construction of the proposed East London River Crossing, thereby preventing the destruction of Oxleas Wood.

Greenwich abounds in opportunities to create more aesthetically pleasing green spaces which also encourage biodiversity. The University of Greenwich, in the centre of Greenwich, offers degrees in landscape architecture and their rooftop gardens at the library on Stockwell Street are an example of biodiversity, practicality and aesthetic pleasure. How fortunate the Council is to have recourse to all this knowledge which could easily be incorporated in existing parks and new housing developments.

Active Friends groups will be vital in a period of diminished funding. They make a huge and visible difference to parks, and the council is heavily dependent on their voluntary work. The Tarn is stunning, Horn Park's new woodlands will one day be very beautiful, and Fairoak Drive Green in the private development at Eltham Heights is closely guarded. Plumstead Common relies on a hardworking group of Friends, and the garden at Charlton House has been created by Friends. Mycenae House Gardens and Hornfair Park are being rescued by Friends.

It is curious therefore that the council does not employ an Ecology Regeneration Manager or a Head of Horticulture to guide the efforts of such committed volunteers.

"Civic pride can, perhaps, be inculcated to a greater degree by the parks department than by any other."[2] Safeguarding what we have depends on practical horticultural knowledge, knowledge of how to deal with climate change and knowledge of new research. But it also needs a vision of what is good for society based on that knowledge, the courage to follow that vision and the strength to lead people towards it. To merely say 'we have done what people wanted' doesn't seem quite good enough.

"Conservation — of all living creatures, including trees — has little chance of long-term success without understanding, which depends in large measure on excellent science. But conservation cannot even get on to the agenda unless people care."[3] This puts responsibility firmly on the shoulders of leaders, including councils, who have the power to guide appropriate and imaginative actions.

Managing the balance between social needs and good living conditions and our need for nature is challenging, but challenges are opportunities to do better, are they not?

MAPS OF AREAS & SITES IN ROYAL BOROUGH OF GREENWICH (RBG)

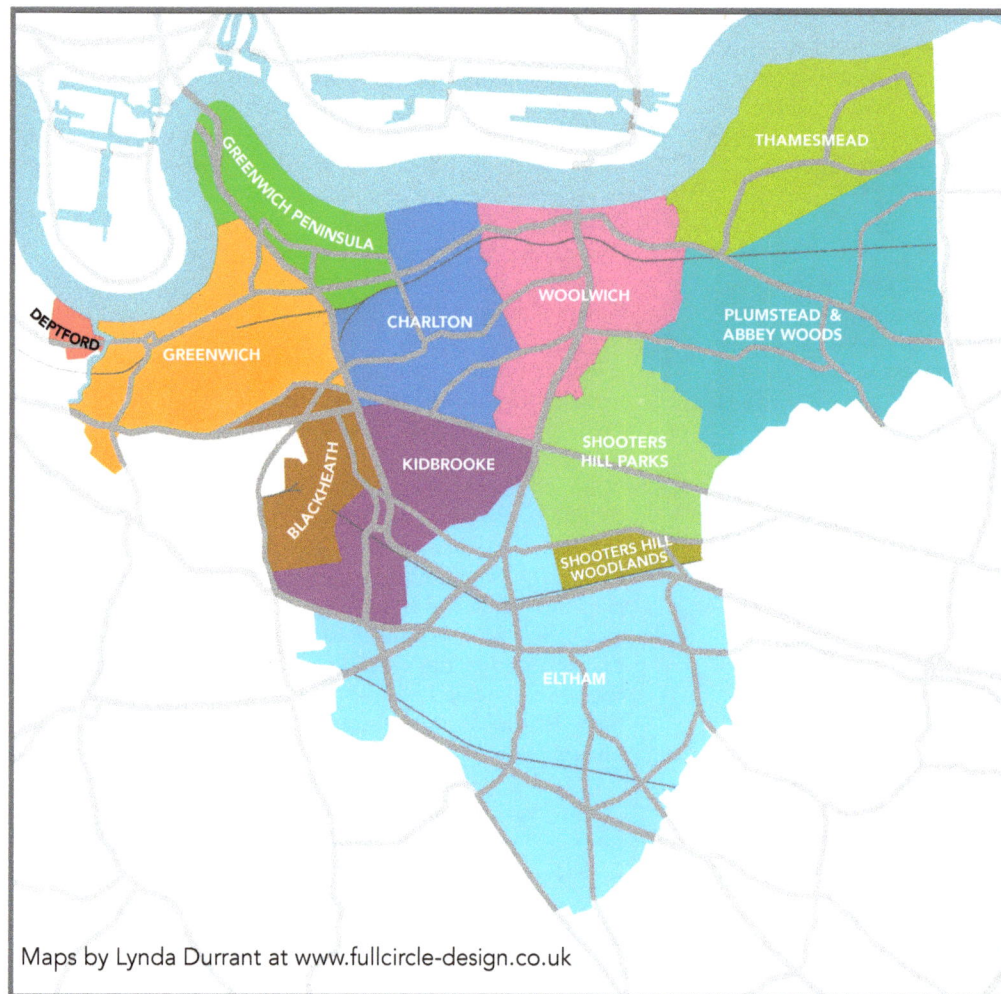

Maps by Lynda Durrant at www.fullcircle-design.co.uk

The sites in RBG are placed in the areas shown above for the purposes of this book; they are not the same as voting areas or administration wards.

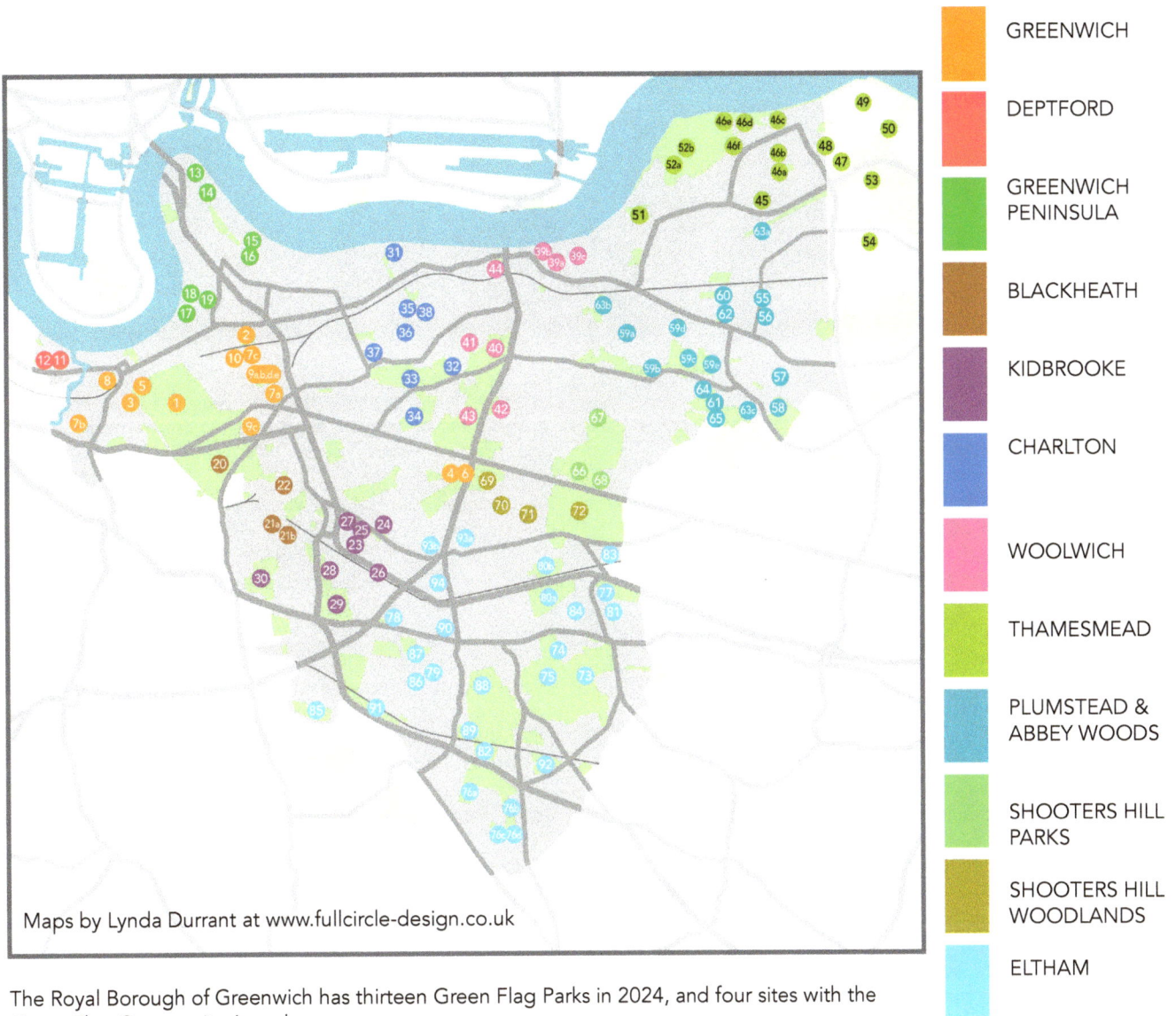

Maps by Lynda Durrant at www.fullcircle-design.co.uk

Legend:
- GREENWICH
- DEPTFORD
- GREENWICH PENINSULA
- BLACKHEATH
- KIDBROOKE
- CHARLTON
- WOOLWICH
- THAMESMEAD
- PLUMSTEAD & ABBEY WOODS
- SHOOTERS HILL PARKS
- SHOOTERS HILL WOODLANDS
- ELTHAM

The Royal Borough of Greenwich has thirteen Green Flag Parks in 2024, and four sites with the Green Flag Community Award.

In London in Bloom, 2024, RBG parks won six Gold Medals, four Outstanding Commendations, the Judges Award and the Outstanding Achievement Award.

THE RIVERS

The Thames

The tidal Thames from Teddington Lock downstream is a SINC (Site of Importance for Nature Conservation) of Metropolitan Importance, with 13 kms of river frontage in the Royal Borough of Greenwich.

In the past, the marshes along the river flooded regularly, and in 1325, a commission was set up to enforce the maintenance of the river walls and drainage ditches from Greenwich to Dartford. The river walls were probably built over hundreds of years in a piecemeal way with a process known as 'inning' and the reclaimed land could then be used to graze sheep and cattle.

The wallscot tax on landowners was introduced in 1527 to fund the flood defence system, and by the early 1600s the most important drainage ditches were in place. But in the 16th century the sea wall was breached several times and 2,000 acres in Erith, Plumstead and Lesnes were flooded for over thirty years. And again "In the year 1671, a great inundation happened at and near Deptford. About 700 sheep, with a great number of oxen, cows, &c. were destroyed in the marshes; the cables of ships at anchor were broken, and the water rose to the height of ten feet in the streets near the river."[4]

The Thames Barrier opened in May 1984 and today protects Central London from flooding by tidal surges.

However, the river levels rise each year, and by 2040 a decision will be needed on whether to build a new barrier or upgrade the existing one.

For centuries, the Thames was an important trade route and London was a major port. In 1599, the Lord Mayor of London and City Merchants established the East India Company at Blackwall, and by the mid-1700s the company dealt with half the world's trade.

Fishing was once an important industry. In Roman times the biggest oyster beds were in the Thames Estuary and oysters were brought to London live, or pickled. "What should I speak of the fat and sweet Salmons daily taken in this Stream, and that in such Plenty, (after the Time of the Smelt is past) as no River in Europe is able to exceed it? But what Store also of Barbels, Trowts, Chevins, Pearches, Smelts, Breams, Roches, Daces, Gudgeons, Flounders, Shrimps, Eeles, &c. are commonly to be had therein," says John Strype in 1603.[5] Only two hundred years ago Woolwich and Barking were significant fishing villages, trading in salmon.

But in the 19th century, the growth of the population, discharge of raw sewage, and the Industrial Revolution started destroying the river. In the Great Stink of 1858, people were actually driven out of London. Nevertheless, fishing for whitebait continued and whitebait suppers were particularly famous in the Trafalgar Tavern.

The river was declared biologically dead in 1957, but it was only from the 1970s that action was taken and organisations such as the National Rivers Authority established. However, the ecological state of the Thames is only deemed to be 'moderate.'

Today, 125 varieties of fish have been recorded, including seabass, eels and smelts, although the salmon have not returned. Seals are fairly common, but ongoing vigilance is needed because the amount of plastic dumped into the river increases every year and sewage discharges remain problematic. A new drainage system, the Tideway Tunnel will be completed in 2025 and it is hoped this drain will have a major impact on the cleanliness of the river.

The Thames is almost a canal now, rigorously contained by embankments and mainly lined with housing from Central London to Erith. The Uber taxis and pleasure steamers cruise the river, with yachting enthusiasts, the occasional cruise liner or naval vessel and the river police. The wildlife has increased, but it is a long way from supporting the fishing industry of past centuries. Nevertheless, the change over the past sixty years has been dramatic.

The Quaggy

The Quaggy, a tributary of the River Ravensbourne, flows for 17 kms through Bromley, Lewisham and Greenwich and has many of its own tributaries.

In Greenwich, we find the Upper, Middle and Lower Kidbrook, the Well Hall Stream and the Little Quaggy. It is a complicated little river, so I refer you to Ken White's excellent booklet for the full story.

Both the Ravensbourne and the Quaggy are prone to flooding, and for many years the river was culverted because it was believed that containing the water and allowing it to rush to a major outlet prevented flooding. This didn't work, and the Quaggy Waterways Action Group has been the driving force in opening up the river and returning it to a natural state with small flood plains and meanders. The volume of water spreads out along the length of the river, habitats for wildlife and appropriate plants are created, and people enjoy the natural beauty.

Sutcliffe Park is a large–scale example of river restoration and the proposed Quaggy River Trail from Sutcliffe Park to the centre of Lee Green could be an exciting continuation. Hints of the river are in the Casterbridge Pond in Blackheath, King George's Field, Well Hall Pleasaunce, The Tarn and the lower end of the Sidcup Grasslands.

The Plumstead River

The River Wogebourne or Woghbourne appears in 14th century manuscripts and later was known as the Plumstead River. However, by the 1970s most of the stream was culverted and renamed the Wickham Valley Waterway.

The stream rises on the eastern slopes of Oxleas Wood and emerges on the northern side of Shooters Hill Road and runs through the Woodlands Trust Farm. From there, it runs across East Wickham Open Space and appears on the eastern side of Wickham Lane opposite Bournewood Road. The stream doglegs down Wickham Lane and then seems to branch.

One branch feeds into Southmere in Thamesmead and then into the Thames via the system of canals. Another branch was uncovered and rerouted during Crossrail building works in Plumstead marshes, but the course of the river is unclear, although it is known to discharge into the drainage canals and lakes in Thamesmead.

Essential reading:

Ackroyd, Peter, *Thames, Sacred River,* (2007, The Book People)
Port of London Authority: www.pla.co.uk/Environment/Nature
Stone, Peter, *The History of the Port of London*, (2017, Pen and Sword)
White, Ken, *The Quaggy River and its Catchment Area,* (1999, Quaggy Waterways Action Group)
A Spark in your Veins, https://e-shootershill.co.uk/2013/09/08/wogebourne/

GREENWICH

It is hard to imagine East Greenwich in the past. The Cantiaci tribe of Iron Age settlers were followed by the Romans from the 1st to 5th centuries AD. And the Romans were followed by the mixed group of people known as Anglo–Saxons, including the Jutes, who landed their boats on the firm and gravelly banks of the Thames and traded from them in beach markets. The Ravensbourne was their route inland. They built houses in the area and their graves are on the hill in Greenwich Park.

It is said that King Alfred's youngest daughter, Princess Aelfrida, gave the Manor of Lewisham (which included East Greenwich, Woolwich, Mottingham and Combe in Kent) to the Abbey of St Peter in Ghent in 918. The manor was administered locally and only returned to English ownership when Henry V repossessed the Alien Priories in 1414.

The Danes continued to raid during the 10th and 11th centuries, but on the whole, life was probably uneventful for ordinary folk living in Gronewic, the Anglo–Saxon name meaning a green landing place or trading place.

Until the mid–1800s, East Greenwich was the great complex of the palace buildings and park surrounded by countryside with farms and large country houses. It was the advent of the railways in 1838 and the opening of Greenwich Station, the first commuter station in London, which escalated development. To the east and on the peninsula, Morden College built housing in the 19th century; Eastcombe Farm was sold for housing, and the Angerstein family sold off Westcombe and the Woodlands Estate, leaving only very small green spaces.

Royal Greenwich

The heyday of Greenwich was the time of the Tudors and the Stuarts in the 15th–17th centuries. There are many books on the subject so only a brief outline is given here.

Humphrey, the Duke of Gloucester, built Bella Court in Greenwich in the 15th century and later enclosed 200 acres of common land as Greenwich Park, with a tower on top of the hill. The palace had a great garden, a little garden and an orchard.

Henry VII demolished Bella Court and built the Greenwich Palace where Henry VIII was born. This palace also had extensive gardens. Elizabeth I commissioned more work in the gardens, including arbours and decorative fountains by her Master Mason, Cornelius Cure.

James I preferred to live in Westminster, but Queen Anne favoured Greenwich. She engaged Salomon de Caus to design a garden at Greenwich and he was paid for making a knot garden in 1613. No plans remain, only the accounts of visitors who talked of parterres, a fountain, a grotto, statuary and bird house. In 1616, Inigo Jones started work on the Queen's House, but Queen Anne died in 1618 and the work on the house was only resumed by Queen Henrietta Maria in 1630. Today it is Grade I listed.

There is no information about the original garden, but from Queen Henrietta Maria's time onwards it is possible the Queen's House had a formal garden on the north side with fountains and straight paths between parterres, beds of flowers and fruit trees. Over time, and with changing needs and fashions, this garden disappeared.

Charles II started building a new palace overlooking the Thames in a completely different style, and in 1694 William and Mary completed the project and established the Royal Hospital for Seamen on the site.

The first graveyard for the hospital, 1707–49, was on the site of 32–40 Maze Hill. The second site was opened on Goddard's Ground, the space which is now partly covered by Devonport House. As many as 20,000 former seamen and marines of the RN were buried here between 1749 and 1856. A mausoleum for senior officers remains on the site, and burials included Sir Thomas Hardy, Nelson's flag captain on Victory at Trafalgar, and Admiral Lord Hood. Both men were also Governors of the Hospital. In 1856 a third burial site was opened at today's East Greenwich Pleasaunce.

From 1869 to 1998 the Hospital was the Royal Naval College and a training establishment for middle–management officers in the RN. The buildings are still in use and today they house the University of Greenwich and Trinity Laban College.

Painted Hall (L) and
King Charles building (R) in
the former Royal Naval College

Above: *The National Maritime Museum, and observatory on the hill*
Below: *Mausoleum in the former Greenwich Hospital Cemetery*

Opposite: *The Long Border behind the Queen's House and the National Maritime Museum*

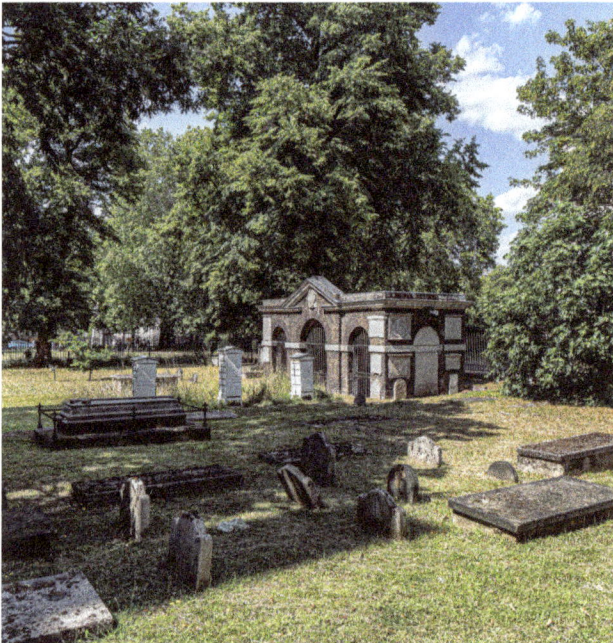

The Queen's House is part of the National Maritime Museum which was set up in the former Royal Hospital School in 1934, and is Grade I listed. A ha–ha which separated the house from the park was replaced with a herbaceous border in 1925. It is the longest in London at 200 metres, and in 2013 it was redesigned by Chris Beardshaw and divided into colour–specific sections by yew hedges.

Essential reading:

Aslet, Clive, *The Story of Greenwich*, (1999, Fourth Estate Limited

Barker, Felix, *Greenwich and Blackheath Past*, (1993, Historical Publications)

Van der Merwe, Pieter, *Royal Greenwich, A History in Kings and Queens*, (2020, National Maritime Museum)

Watson, Julian, and Gregory, Kit, *In the Meantime*, (1988, London Borough of Greenwich Tourism Section)

Greenwich Park

1

Greenwich Park is part of the UNESCO World Heritage Site which includes the National Maritime Museum, the Queen's House, and the former Royal Naval College.

The park lies on the flat London clay along the river and rises up the side of the escarpment to the gravel beds of Blackheath. It is the oldest enclosed Royal Park. Originally it was heath and woodland, but in the 16th century Henry VIII introduced deer for hunting. In the next century, James I enclosed the park with a brick wall which remains in place today and is Grade II listed. The Royal Observatory was built in 1675.

Today's landscape was developed by Charles II, who was influenced by his years of exile in France, and it seems to be the work of several people.

Sir William Boreman, Clerk to the Royal household, implemented the King's plans in the park. In 1661, he started planting the Wilderness, mixed woodlands on the southern boundary of the park. Long avenues were planted in there with 6,000 elms and many Spanish chestnuts; 600 of the chestnuts came from Lesnes Abbey. It is possible that the layout of the avenues was influenced by Claude Mollet,

who had worked for James I, and his son, André, who worked for Charles I.

Even in 1912, Sir Walter Besant could write, "The Avenues are lined with magnificent elms, many of which ... were planted in 1664."[6] Sadly, the elms were destroyed in the 1970s by Dutch Elm Disease, and now many of the old chestnut trees are also succumbing to disease.

The Queen's Orchard, which still has an original black mulberry tree, was the work of Sir William as well. The site was used as allotments in WWII and then neglected until reopening in 2013 with the help of volunteers and friends as a delightful vegetable and fruit garden along Park Vista.

But the King also wanted a cascade down the hill, perhaps similar to what he had seen in France during his exile. In 1661, twelve levels of steps were cut into the hillside by Sir William Boreman, sloping down from the tower on top of the hill and lined up with the Queen's House. Each was forty yards wide and there were hawthorn or pine trees on both sides. However, there was no easy source of water. Le Nôtre was suggested as someone who might complete the scheme.

Looking towards the Observatory and the new giant steps

Le Nôtre planned a flat parterre on the south side of the Queen's House leading to a grotto. There were to be three fountains and avenues of trees on either side. The ground was levelled, but a few years later the idea of a water cascade was abandoned and the parterre was not made either, although hundreds of elm and lime trees were planted in avenues.

The Victorian tradition continues in the Flower Garden with circular beds of annuals amongst stately trees such as cedars of Lebanon and tulip trees. And the park has recently been transformed again.

'Greenwich Revealed' was a four-year restoration project which cost £8 million and completed in 2024. The project replaced dying trees in the historic avenues, restored the grand ascent (commonly known as the giant steps) and parterre banks, and created new visitor facilities, a new café and education centre, and refurbished the lake, amongst other improvements. A herb garden is at St Mary's Gate, and the 19th century Dell Garden, which was originally planted in a former gravel pit with acid–loving plants, has now been changed to a seating area. Surveys have been conducted, and in the future the management aims to increase biodiversity.

These are bare facts about the park, but they don't tell you about the glorious views over the Thames at dawn, or at sunset, the squeaking of the ring–necked parakeets, the cheeky squirrels, the scents of flowering shrubs and chestnut trees in the spring, or the exquisitely moulded camellia and magnolia blooms. And they give no hint of the real glory of the park — the c.4,000 trees of which fifty–two sweet chestnuts, eight oaks, one sycamore and a cedar are Ancient and Veteran trees. (There is a helpful tree trail on the Friends' website.) Gnarled and broken chestnut trees and oak trees endure: massive, solid trunks that have seen the centuries pass and still manage to support life for another year, 'food for the soul' which sets us an example, and gives hope.

Access: Entrances into the park on all sides from Charlton Way, Crooms Hill, Maze Hill and King William's Walk
Opening times: Dawn to dusk (check website); Queen's Orchard opening times on website but unreliable
Facilities: Observatory, Flamsteed House, cafés, toilets, children's playground, boating lake, cricket pitch, tennis courts, paying car park, education centre
Designation: SINC of Metropolitan Importance, World Heritage Site, Grade I listed, Green Flag Public Park
Size: 77 hectares (190 acres)
Greenwich Park: www.royalparks.org.uk/parks/greenwich-park
Friends of Greenwich Park: www.friendsofgreenwichpark.org.uk

A reminder of the wonderful magnolia trees
which once flourished in the park

The camellias in late February

The Queen's Orchard

East Greenwich Pleasaunce

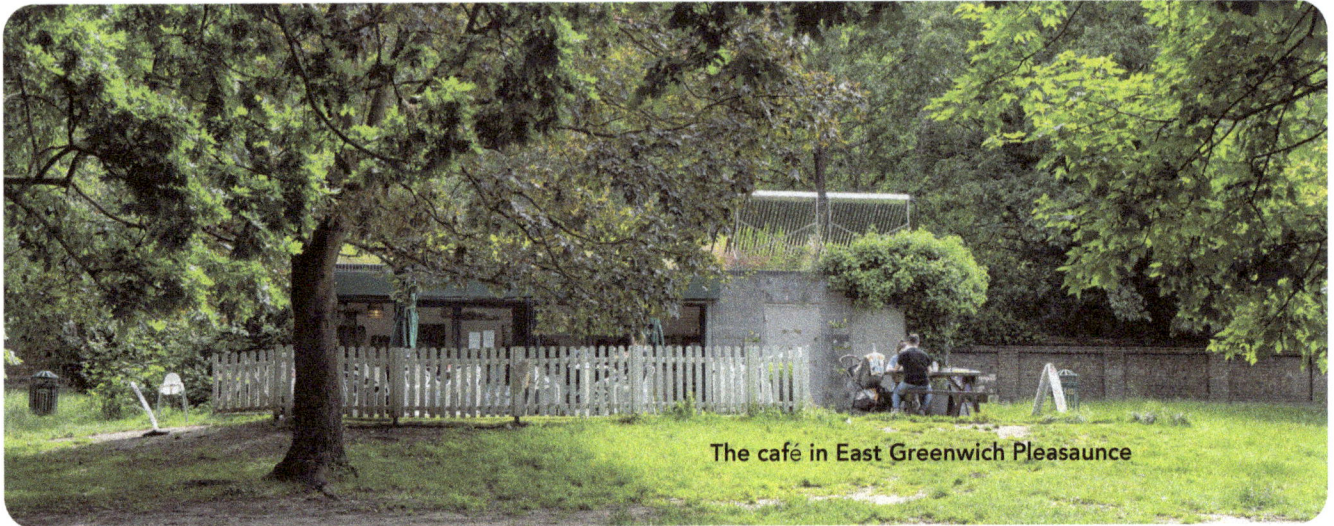

The café in East Greenwich Pleasaunce

The East Greenwich Pleasaunce is a curious site — part graveyard, and part park, with a children's playground and café.

Today's park is the third and final graveyard for the Royal Naval Hospital in Greenwich. When the first two graveyards were full, the Hospital Commissioners bought land (formerly orchards) from the trustees of the late Sir Gregory Page–Turner, and the new cemetery opened in 1857.

In 1875, the remains of 3,000 former pensioners buried in Goddard's Ground were reburied in the new cemetery. More graves were moved when Devonport House was built in Central Greenwich in 1924. The officers were buried in a fenced plot, separated from the seamen. There are also CWGC (Commonwealth War Grave Commission) graves here: twenty from WWI and two from WWII.

The burial ground was sold to Greenwich Borough Council in 1926, railings were removed and the site was re–landscaped as a park, although the last burial was only in 1981.

There are at least 120 trees in the park: birches, pleached lime trees along the walls, holly, ash, two beautiful mature holm oaks in the children's play area, a black poplar, and firs and pine trees amongst others in the woodland. And a small community orchard planted in 2010 grows apples, pears and plums. The Bridge is a community hub, and Pistachios in the Park offers delicious refreshments in an eco–friendly building designed by Alexander Sedgeley Architects.

2

I feel uneasy about dogs and children playing amongst the graves because it seems disrespectful to the dead, especially those killed in war, and prefer the calm of Brockley Cemetery in Lewisham, where the dead seem to rest easy. But perhaps you think that we the living should be more realistic and make death part of our ordinary, everyday life?

And wouldn't it be wonderful if the graves were surrounded by wildflowers and bulbs, and the woodland area was a carpet of crocuses in early spring, with the greenery under the trees protected by deadhedging?

Access: Chevening Road SE10 0LB,
Halstow Road SE10 0LD
Opening times: 8.30 am to dusk
Facilities: Children's playground, community hub,
community orchard, café, toilets
Designation: Green Flag Public Park
Size: 2.4 hectares (6 acres)

War graves in the park, and the woodland area

Gloucester Circus

3

The glory of the garden is the trees — three magnificent London plane trees, a copper beech, Norway maple, tulip tree and mulberry tree, amongst others, stand in the square. Shrubs and roses line the railings and the centre offers an expanse of peaceful lawn. Do visit on an Open Day.

Gloucester Circus (1791–1809) was designed by Michael Searles, the architect of the Paragon in Blackheath. Apparently he wanted to create an oval circus, but the north side was not completed and it remains semi–circular. The houses on the southern side are Grade II listed; those on the north are council properties.

The garden is enclosed by railings and is privately owned by the residents who pay for the maintenance of the square.

Access: Gloucester Circus SE10 8RY
Opening times: Only open to the public on special occasions
Designation: Private Park
Size: 0.4 hectares (1 acre)

Tulip tree (above) and the central lawn in June (opposite)

Greenwich Cemetery

4

A dramatic War Memorial crowns the crest of the hill in Greenwich Cemetery. Its two curved walls record the names of those buried in the cemetery, and behind the wall, 263 service people are interred in Heroes Corner. The CWGC lists 715 war dead in the cemetery of which 561 are from WWI and 124 from WWII. Some Kipling stones are grouped near the crest of the hill, others stand with family members.

Thirty Norwegian service people and refugees from World War II rest in a carefully tended plot in the western corner of the cemetery.

The cemetery was laid out in 1856 by the Greenwich Burial Board on sixteen acres of hillside with sweeping views over London. In 1905, the Burial Board bought a further six acres from the Earl of St Germans. There are two Gothic chapels and a 1930s lodge at the entrance.

But this cemetery is also a nature park.

From the entrance, take a path along the boundary, past mature lime trees, horse chestnuts, oaks, some yews, pines and Leylandii, and through areas which are managed as conservation grassland. The London clay and neutral grassland, which is unusual in London, support a variety of wildflowers and grasses including Pignut and Lady's Bedstraw, and attract wildlife. And there are several springs.

Burial grounds can be interesting places for biodiversity because they are left undisturbed: the walls and the monuments encourage mosses, ferns and lichens while the richness of the plants support small animals, insects and birds.

The wilder areas of the cemetery are particularly beautiful. Do walk here, especially in the spring when you will find swathes of crocuses.

Access: Well Hall Road SE9 6UA
Opening times: 9.00 am to 4.00 pm winter;
9.00 am to 7.00 pm summer
Facilities: Toilets, car park outside the gate
Designation: Cemetery, SINC Borough Importance Grade I
Size: 9.1 hectares (22.5 acres)

Greenwich University Roof Gardens

Greenwich University has an interesting new building on Stockwell Street in the centre of Greenwich, designed by Heneghan Peng, architects specialising in design programmes. The new buildings, which opened in 2014 and house a library, design, TV and film studios, won a RIBA National Award and a RIBA London Regional Award in 2015.

But the most interesting aspect is the green roofs, which were awarded a prized innovation credit for sustainability. They comprise fourteen stepped terraces forming one of the largest multi–functional green roofs in the world.

"Roofs and facades need to do more than keeping the weather out, and our green roofs are exemplars in using nature–based solutions in reducing the urban heat island effect and growing food, including fish and vegetables, in our Aquaponics Labs, providing better food security and the reduction in food miles and ecological footprints," says Dr Benz Kotzen, Professor of Landscape Architecture and Nature–Based Solutions.

The roofs step downwards so that residents are not overshadowed. They include a potager vegetable garden, fruit trees, hedges, lawns, wildflower meadows, and ponds, as well as beehives. They are beautiful to look at but also provide teaching spaces and specialist research environments for the study of plants, algae and aquaponics.

On the first floor is a huge internal living green wall. The plants take in carbon dioxide and release oxygen during photosynthesis. This helps to keep the air fresh inside the building — I found I was smiling just by looking at the lush greenery as I walked past.

And now my home has a large plant in every window.

Access: Stockwell Street SE10 9BD
Opening times: Not open to the public; access for groups can be arranged (b.kotzen@gre.ac.uk)
Size: 0.5 hectares (c.1.5 acres)
University of Greenwich: https://www.gre.ac.uk/about-us/travel/greenwich/stockwell

5

King George's Field

6

The field alongside the Greenwich Cemetery was once common land and part of Eltham Common and Woolwich Common. The council bought the field from the War Department in 1952 with the help of a donation from King George's Fields Foundation.

This is rather a complicated story of three very similar charities!

The National Playing Fields Foundation was founded in 1925 by the Duke of York, later King George VI, who was the first president. Grants were available to fund playing fields across the UK, with the stipulation that they be called "King George's Field and [display] a pair of heraldic panels or similar signage to remember the king."[7] The overriding aim was to engage children in play and sport to benefit their health and general well–being.

The King George's Fields Foundation dates from 1936 after the death of George V, and was set up in his memory to be independent of the National Playing Fields Foundation but with very similar aims. The foundation closed down in 1965 when all the funds had been allocated.

During its time, 471 King George's Fields had been created in the UK and the National Playing Fields Association (NPFA) then took over responsibility for the sites.

The National Playing Fields Foundation changed its name to Fields in Trust in 2008.

King George's Field below Shooters Hill is open grassland with mature oak trees in the middle of the field and a young redwood near the commemorative brick structure. The narrow ditch along the boundary with the cemetery is marked by some beautiful willow trees and carries the Lower Kidbrook.

King George's Field is a beautiful open field, but rather than an area for sporting activity, it is perhaps a space for contemplation and quietness, a pause between the cemetery and the present moment.

Access: Broad Walk SE9 6TZ
Opening times: Always open
Facilities: Litter bins, seating in the brick niche/name wall
Designation: Amenity Green Space
Size: 2 hectares (4.94 acres)

Little Corners

Batley Park SE3 7HB

Batley Park is intriguing! On John Rocque's map of 1761, this park at the Blackheath Standard is Sheepgate Green. The OS map of 1870–82 shows a pond, so drovers could have watered their animals here. And were they travelling to and from grazing on the former marshes? From here, Coombe Farm Lane (Westcombe Hill) leads down to the Woolwich Road and the river.

By the late 1800s, houses were springing up in the surrounding area, and William Fox Batley, a corn merchant by trade, and other local dignitaries campaigned to smarten the little park with railings, toilets and trees. Today, the railings remain, the trees have matured and spring bulbs are followed by wildflowers in the unmown half of the park. Do stop and linger for a while and then relax with coffee and cake at the delightful Mara Café.

Catherine Grove SE10 8BS

Catherine Grove is a pocket park which was once in the grounds of Catherine House, a late 18th century Grade II listed building at 31 Blackheath Road. Morden College owned the land and started building houses in the area in the mid–1800s, including on Catherine House grounds.

During WWII, the housing here was badly damaged and the grove became a rubbish dump. By 2006, local residents decided enough was enough and, with council funding, started today's little garden, which hides away from the constant stream of traffic heading to and from Blackheath.

Humber Road Allotments SE3 7LR

These delightful allotments with views towards the City are a green haven in a densely built–up area. The area was once part of the Westcombe Estate and the road was named after William Humber, a Director of the Westcombe Park Estate Company which bought the Woodlands and Westcombe Estates to build houses.

7a
7b
7c

Below: Batley Park, Community Open Space of 0.4 hectares (1 acre), Charlton Road, always open

Above: *Catherine Grove, Public Park of 0.08 hectares (0.2 acres), always open*
Below: *Humber Road Allotments, Community Space of 0.4 hectaress (1 acre), not open to the public*

St Alfege Church & Park

Step off the pavement in the middle of Greenwich and walk down St Alfege Passage next to the church towards a gate in a far wall. You will find yourself in a secret garden with mature trees, quiet and peaceful, and away from the tourists who crowd the busy town centre just yards away.

The church is named after St Alfege, an Archbishop of Canterbury. He was captured by the Vikings in 1017 and taken to Greenwich in the hope of a large ransom, but the Archbishop refused to be ransomed and was brutally murdered. It is believed the first church here was built on the site of his martyrdom.

St Alfege was rebuilt in the late 13th century but damaged by a catastrophic storm in 1710. Today's church is the third on the site, a Grade I listed building designed by Nicholas Hawksmoor and rebuilt in 1712–14 under the Fifty New Churches Act. The mediaeval tower was retained, and recased, and the church was reconsecrated in 1718. Further restoration was needed to repair considerable damage during WWII.

The churchyard was enlarged in 1716, 1774 and 1808, but by 1853 the graveyard was full and closed for burials. The new Greenwich Cemetery opened at the foot of Shooters Hill three years later.

The extended churchyard was laid out in 1889 as a public garden and recreation ground by Fanny Wilkinson, the Head Gardener of the Metropolitan Public Gardens Association, and opened by HRH The Duke of Cambridge. Sadly, her original plans for the garden have disappeared.

Several notable people are buried in or around the church: Thomas Tallis (d.1585) was buried under the mediaeval church, and General James Wolfe (d.1759) and John Julius Angerstein (d.1823) are buried in the crypt in family vaults.

Above: *Stained glass window in St Alfege Church commemorating General James Wolfe*
Opposite: *St Alfege Park*

Access: Greenwich Church Street SE10 9RB
Opening times: 9 am to dusk
Facilities: Benches, children's playground, ball court
Designation: Churchyard and Park
Size: Churchyard and Public Park, 1.3 hectares (3.2 acres)
St Alfege Church: www.st-alfege.org.uk

Woodlands Estate

Woodlands, now a Steiner school

Woodlands & Mycenae House Gardens

John Julius Angerstein was born in Russia c.1732 and as a teenager came to London where he worked for Andrew Poulett Thomson. He was smart, became a broker and made a fortune in marine insurance. Anderstein was a founder of Lloyds, and its Chairman from 1790–96. He was also an art collector, and thirty–eight European Old Masters' paintings from his collection formed the nucleus of the National Gallery collection after his death.

In 1774, Angerstein leased a forty–one–acre farm from Sir Gregory Page and two years later built Woodlands as his country villa; today it is Grade II* listed. George Gibson the Younger, who built Stone House and renovated St Mary's Church in Lewisham, was the architect.

Woodlands was originally a modest villa, opening on the east side and set in parklands. Daniel Lysons wrote, in 1796, that the mansion "occupies a situation uncommonly beautiful. The surrounding scenery is very picturesque; and the distant view of the river, and the Essex shore, is broken with good effect by the plantations near the house... The greenhouse is to be remarked for its collection of [Cape] heaths."[8] The greenhouse was 300'x50', and there was also a four–acre kitchen garden, hothouses, grotto, a dairy and a farmyard with water. In the grounds was an icehouse.

David Stewart, one of the foremost gardeners of his time, was the head gardener, and his successor was Robert Sweet, who described the greenhouse as "walking in an evergreen flowery wood... [with] the choicest and newest plants from China, New Holland, the Cape of Good Hope."[9] There were even trees: "in the centre [of the conservatory] stands a superb and lofty pine from Van Diemen's Land for which Mr Angerstein was once offered a thousand guineas."[10] No wonder the conservatory was used for elaborate entertaining!

The stately avenue of five London plane trees may date from the 18th century; four of the trees are listed on the Ancient Tree Inventory as Notable and one is a Veteran. London plane trees, a hybrid of an American sycamore and an Oriental plane, were first discovered in the 1600s by John Tradescant and widely planted in London from the 1700s. The line of plane trees continues in Woodland Dell. Even in 1882, F H Hart found a fine garden with "one of the most extensive collections of azaleas, rhododendrons, heaths, and curious plants, in the kingdom."[11]

Angerstein increased his property by buying c.131 acres of the East Combe estate from the Crown in 1802, and in the same year he illegally enclosed twenty–six acres of manorial waste on Blackheath, making the parish an annual donation in response to local protest.

The lease expired in 1873, and the Page–Turner family sold part of the estate to the Westcombe Park Estate Company for new roads and new housing. Woodlands and some of its land remained in private ownership. In the 1920s, the Little Sisters of the Assumption bought Woodlands, sold more ground, and in 1933 built a new novitiate house.

The property passed in 1967 to the RBG, which converted Woodlands into an art gallery and local history library. The novitiate house became a community centre named Mycenae House, managed by the Vanbrugh Community Association from 1994.

In 2006, Woodlands was converted into a Steiner School, which created a dilemma. Children need schools, and school children want an open space in which to play, but what about the garden? The ground under the trees is bare and the grass damaged by overuse. Several beds have been fenced off to encourage regrowth and investigations are ongoing for suitable plants. This garden presents a considerable challenge to the skills and ingenuity of the redoubtable Friends!

Access: Mycenae Road SE3 7SE
Opening times: Always open
Designation: Community Amenity Space, SINC of Local Importance
Size: 1.3 hectares (3.2 acres) for Mycenae Gardens & Dell Friends of Mycenae Gardens and Woodlands Dell: https://mycenaegardens.org.uk

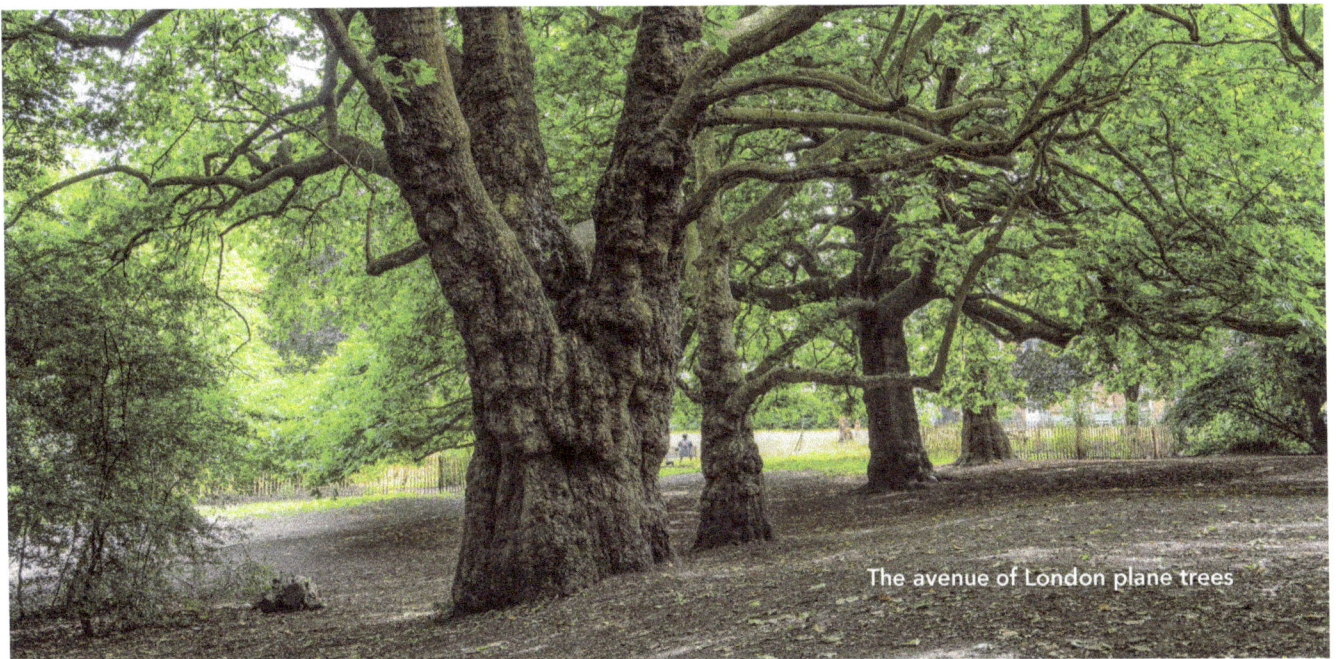

The avenue of London plane trees

Westcombe Woodland Dell

The Dell was once part of the gardens of Woodlands, but now the two sites are separated by a wall and have each developed their own character.

The Dell is unexpected, even mysterious: dense woodland with a very fine old ash tree in the middle where there is also the remains of a large pond, clearly visible on the OS map of 1870. The pond was later in the grounds of Fairfax House on Beaconsfield Road.

Old Christmas trees are used for deadhedging here, marking the path and protecting the wildflowers — a splendid, cheap idea implemented by one of the local residents.

Access: Mycenae Road SE3 7SG
Opening times: Always open
Facilities: None
Designation: Community Open Space, SINC of Local Importance
Size: 0.4 hectares (1 acre)

The Veteran pedunculate oak which stands in Beaconsfield Crescent may once have been in the grounds of Woodlands, and from the mid-1800s it was on the boundary between Kingsbridge House and Fairfax House.

Frederick Garrard lived in Fairfax House and owned a business in Millwall which made high–quality wall and floor tiles, copies of Spanish and Dutch tiles. He was commissioned to work in Charlton House and his tiles are found in many prominent public buildings.

Access: Beaconsfield Crescent SE3 7LJ

43

Angerstein Lane

Around 1804, Angerstein created a carriageway lined with elm trees from the south gates of Woodlands (on Vanbrugh Park) to Shooters Hill. This may be the origin of Angerstein Lane.

The little lane between the A2 and St John's Park is quite charming, a country lane where Steve Whitefield has fashioned a cottage garden with bulbs, roses and espaliered fruit trees. It is glorious in spring and summer.

The lane is always open and can be accessed from St John's Park SE3 7TT

9c

Above: *Steve Whitefield's garden and some of his roses*
Below: *The entrance to Angerstein Lane*

Vicarage Avenue

Vicarage Avenue was intended as a private road in the Angerstein Estate and a footpath to access St John's Church. In the 1840s, the South Eastern Railway built a mile–long tunnel under the Avenue.

Today, Vicarage Avenue is a pleasant, treed footpath which links Shooters Hill Road to the shops on the Old Dover Road.

Access: St John's Park SE3 7JP
Designation: Amenity Green Space
Size: 0.3 hectares (0.7 acres)

Ingleside Gardens

Ingleside Gardens is a triangular site which was originally intended for a new church in the Westcombe Park development in 1877. But instead, the Church of St George was built in Kirkside Road.

The gardens, potentially a surprising and very pretty little park amongst elegant houses, are sadly neglected with dead trees and unloved shrubs. The council says the garden is maintained by the cleaning team, but where are the gardeners, and the Friends?

Access: Ingleside Grove SE3 7PH
Opening times: Always open
Facilities: Benches
Designation: Community Open Space:
Size: 0.2 hectares (0.5 acres)

9d
9e

Vicarage Avenue

St George's Church

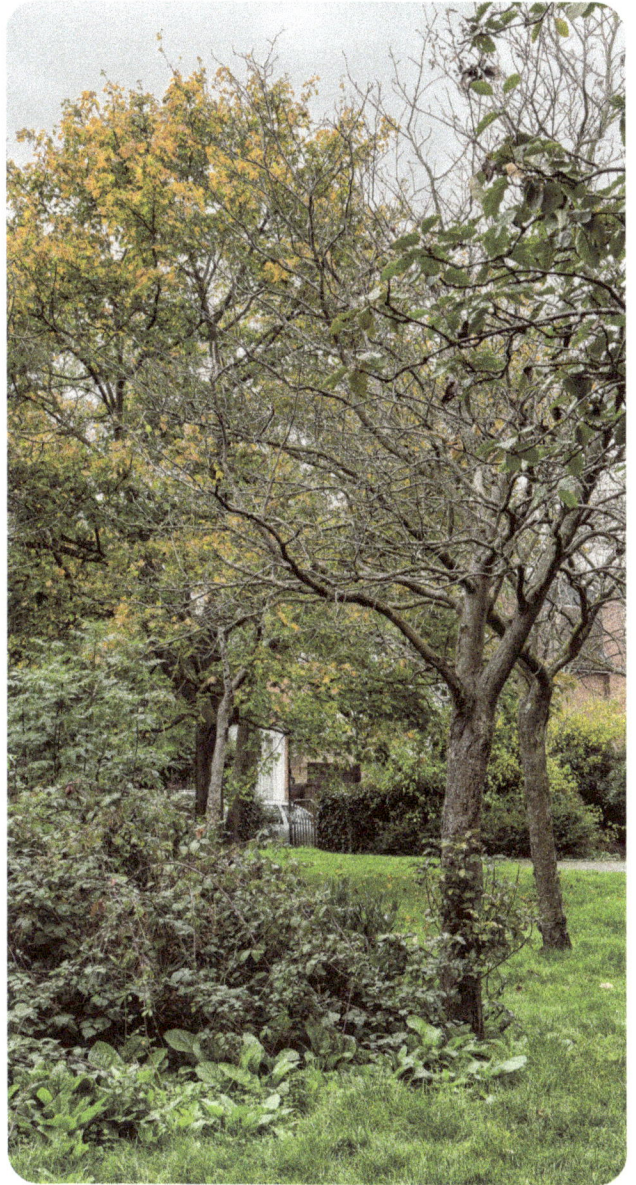

Ingleside Gardens

Westcombe Woodlands

Westcombe Woodlands is a delightful area of secondary woodland on the steep hillside of Maze Hill. Careful management has reduced the shrub layer, allowing diversity, and indigenous trees such as elms have been planted. New nest boxes are encouraging the tawny owl to breed, and a little pond is creating another new habitat.

The woodlands were once a sand and gravel quarry on fields known as Ballast Field or Gravel Pit Field. The gravel was used as ballast for ships, such as the colliers on their return journeys, and chalk may also have been quarried and burned to produce lime. The pits were probably worked from the 1600s until some point in the late 1700s.

In the 1800s, the flatter parts of the area, which were still countryside, were used as allotments, kitchen gardens, pig farms and perhaps for milk cows.

Woodlands House (not Angerstein's property) was on the east of the site and its 19th century lodge still stands at the entrance of Lasseter Close. In 1920, the property was sold to the Greenwich District Hospital, and nurses' accommodation was built. Restell Close and the tower blocks followed in the 1960s.

In 1982, the Blackheath Preservation Trust (BPT) bought the woodlands from the Regional Health Authority to protect the site from development and to preserve it as a safe haven for wildlife. In 2015, the BPT transferred the freehold to the Woodland Trust, who simultaneously granted the Friends of Westcombe Woodlands (a charity) a 999–year lease with the responsibility to actively manage the site.

Do visit on an Open Day!

Access: Restell Close SE3 7RD (steps, steep hillside)
Opening times: Selected open days announced on website
Facilities: None
Designation: SINC of Local Importance Grade II with recommended upgrade to Borough Importance
Size: 2.6 hectares (6.5 acres)
Friends of Westcombe Woodlands:
https://www.westcombewoodlands.uk

Pond dipping

Busy bees!

10

Bluebells at the end of April

New Elm tree

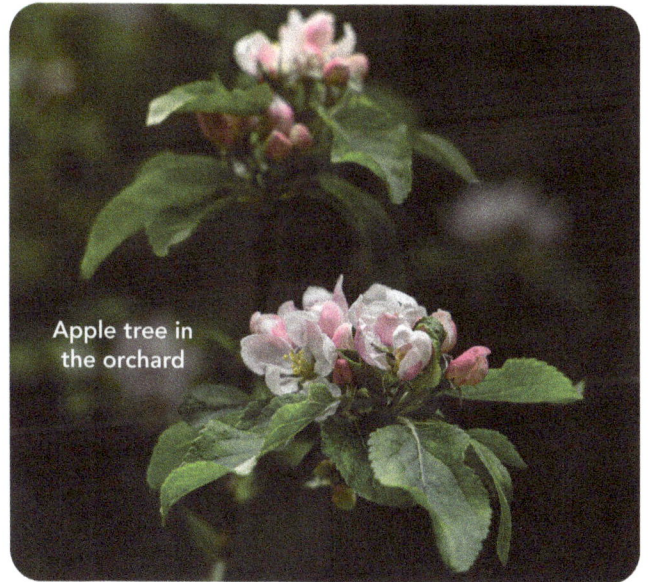

Apple tree in the orchard

DEPTFORD

West Greenwich used to include the thriving community of Deptford. Today, it is just a small area redeveloped from a maze of houses and riverside industries, and the only reminders of everyday life in the past are the Dog and Bell pub and St Nicholas Church.

Essential reading:

Dews, Nathan, *History of Deptford, 1884* (2015, republished by FamLoc, Michael Wood (Editor))

St Nicholas Churchyard

St Nicholas Church comes as a surprise, surrounded by new housing and near the very busy main road into Greenwich. But every time I walk through the gates and inside the encircling walls, I feel I am entering a distant, calmer, and more peaceful world.

A church has stood here for over a thousand years, and today's Grade II* listed building is the third church on the site. It dates from 1697 and was restored in 1958 after bomb damage during WWII. St Nicholas was the parish church until 1730, when the parish was divided and St Paul's was built further to the south to accommodate the increasing population.

The curious skull–and–crossbone carvings on the main gateposts might mean plague victims were buried in the churchyard, or perhaps it was just a Momento Mori?

On the east gates, the three golden balls represent St Nicholas of Bari who gave a dowry of three bags of gold to three girls when their father was about to sell them into prostitution. It is also the sign of pawnbrokers, and St Nicholas is the patron saint of sailors — a curious mixture.

The charnel house or ossuary just inside the main gate is 17th century. When small churchyards became too crowded, or if bones were exposed when new graves were dug, the remains were stored in the ossuary.

Along the sides of the churchyard there are some very old plane trees, holly and some flowering shrubs, but there are also two interesting varieties of fern on the tombstones: rustyback fern and maidenhair spleenwort, although these are disappearing.

The gravestones have mainly disappeared, but those buried here include Captain Edward Fenton, who accompanied Frobisher and then was in action against the Spanish Armada; John Evelyn was a Church Warden and buried two of his children here; the shipwrights Peter Pett, and Jonas Shish and his two sons, John and Thomas, who were all Master Shipwrights at Deptford and Woolwich in the 17th century; and Christopher Marlowe.

Do visit if you don't know St Nicholas.

Access: Deptford Green SE8 3DQ
Opening times: Churchyard is always open
Facilities: Benches
Designation: SINC Borough Importance Grade II
Size: 0.3 hectares (0.75 acres)

Base of original tower

11

Old tombstones

Charlotte Turner Gardens & Twinkle Park

St Nicholas had an additional walled, burial ground on Wellington Street (now McMillan Street) which was consecrated in 1765 but closed a century later.

The Disused Burial Grounds Act came into force in 1884 and, in the same year, the graveyard was laid out as a garden, with a donation from the Kyrle Society. The site was extended to the north in 1897 and widened to the west in the 20th century.

Today this is Charlotte Turner Gardens, an old–fashioned village green with a wide, grassed, central area, winding paths, some stately London plane trees and a Notable golden weeping willow. It is named after Charlotte Turner who was a JP and Mayor of Greenwich 1931–33.

Twinkle Park nearby was created in 1996 from the derelict Hughes Fields Recreation Ground that had provided a council–run swings from the early 1990s, supervised by a Mrs Twinkle!

Greenwich Mural Workshops managed the regeneration project, running workshops with local residents and schools, fundraising and appointing designers. The large pond, and a metal gazebo with a movable seat, separate the pond and its wildlife garden from a floodlit ball games area for general use. The pond is well planted, hosts a shoal of goldfish, and attracts coots, ducks and other wildlife. It is kept in good health by a group of volunteers. The RBG leases the two parks to Twinkle Park Trust who manage the parks with maintenance help from the council.

Access: Charlotte Turner Gardens, Watergate Street SE8 3HY; Twinkle Park, Borthwick Street SE8 3HD
Opening times: Always open
Facilities: Benches, toddlers play area, pétanque court, table tennis, floodlit games area, fitness trail
Designation: Green Flag Public Parks, SINCs of Local Importance
Size: Charlotte Turner Gardens 1.2 hectares (3 acres), Twinkle Park 0.4 hectares (1 acre)

12

Charlotte Turner Gardens

Above and Below: *Twinkle Park*

GREENWICH PENINSULA

Thousands of years ago, Greenwich Peninsula was a series of small islands in marshy ground with reeds, rushes and ferns, and perhaps clumps of alders. As the land rose towards the south oak, lime and hazel trees flourished.

From the Bronze Age onwards there is evidence of wooden trackways across the marshes, perhaps routes to fishing and hunting for Celts, Saxons and Romans living on the drier upland areas. The southern boundary of the marshes was roughly today's Woolwich Road.

By the 17th century, most of the peninsula was owned by charities who leased reclaimed land to support their charitable activities. The biggest landowner until the last century was Morden College. Cattle and horses grazed on the fields, and along the river small businesses included fishing, barge building and of course smuggling.

The big change came in the 1800s, and by the end of the century the whole area was industrialised. Only the market gardens owned by the Mason Brothers remained as a green space in the area of today's yacht club, where the pier was known as Pear Tree Wharf.

The 19th century was a time of remarkable innovation and invention on the peninsula.

An extraordinary range of goods was produced: soap, candles, cement, concrete slabs, small arms armaments, boats, barges, creosote and so on. Coal was the major import and extremely important as it produced domestic energy and powered industry. The by–products of coal created successful chemical industries.

Perhaps most interestingly, the undersea telegraph cable which connected Europe and America was manufactured on the peninsula, at Enderby and Morden Wharves, and carried by the Great Eastern, which was built at Millwall Ironworks on the Isle of Dogs. International cable is still manufactured at Enderby Wharf by Alcatel.

From the 1960s, coal mining declined as cheaper sources of energy were found, e.g. North Sea gas and oil. This contributed hugely to the closure of the London docks in the 1960s–70s. Although some industries continued, large areas of the peninsula quickly became derelict.

'Head in the Wind' by Allen Jones

The Millennium celebrations and the siting of the O2 Arena on the peninsula were the impetus for regeneration through building an entirely new community.

In the north, Knight Dragon is undertaking a thirty–year project costing c.£8.4 billion. It is the biggest regeneration project in Europe and described by the developers as 'New London', "a creative blueprint for the London of the future" and "a progressive London destination [that] will inspire a new concept for urban living."[12]

Will the new Creative District match the 19th century achievements?

Greenwich Peninsula is home to one of the largest collections of public art in London, with pieces by Damien Hirst, Ian Davenport, Morag Myerscough, Antony Gormley and Marwan Kaabour. Architecture in the Design District is imaginative, and residents in the high–rise apartment blocks can connect with nature in The Tide, an elevated linear park and public art trail linking the North Greenwich Station to the river, or the nearby Central Park.

To the south and east, Greenwich Millennium Village Ltd offers residents flats, some around garden squares. Here, the extraordinary Greenwich Ecology Park gives a hint of the original nature of the peninsula, and Southern Park acts as a village green.

On the west bank of the peninsula lie Ballast Quay Garden, River Gardens and Christchurch School Community Garden.

Sadly, there is hardly anything which informs current residents of the industrial history of the area. Change is a natural part of life. However, I agree that "Nothing is old and romantic, but we live among the accretions of the past and we owe it some respect."[13]

Books by Dr Mary Mills are essential reading:

Greenwich Marsh – The 300 years before the Dome, (1999, printed by Biddles)
Greenwich Peninsula, Greenwich Marsh — History of an Industrial Heartland, (2000, printed by Amazon)
The Greenwich Riverside: Watergate to Upper Angerstein, (2021, printed by Amazon)

Above: 'The Mermaid' by Damien Hirst from 'Treasures of the Wreck of the Unbelievable' which was exhibited in the 2017 Venice Biennale. It stands on the river front at the end of The Tide.

The Tide

"The Tide, London's first elevated garden walkway and public art trail that celebrates art, design and wellbeing."[14]

The Tide is planted with grasses, wildflowers and birch trees, and dotted with benches. Terraces on the slope down to the Thames Path are planted with ornamental grasses. Art installations surrounding The Tide are by Damien Hirst, Allen Jones and Morag Myerscough.

13

Central Park
Greenwich Peninsula

14

Central Park, in the middle of the peninsula, is the biggest natural green space open to the public in this area. Desvigne and Dalnoky designed the park for the Millennium celebrations.

Lush green grassland, with groves of trees and swathes of daffodils in the spring, attracts dog walkers and families with children. Sadly, this elegant park lacks the variety of habitats found in the Ecology Park, to the detriment of biodiversity. But it does have its own Georgian pub!

George Russell and his family became wealthy through manufacturing soap at the Old Barge House factory at Blackfriars Bridge (now the Oxo Tower). He then bought land on the Greenwich Marshes and built a Tide Mill on Bugsby's Reach, 1801–04, together with The Pilot Inn and the adjoining cottages, which were probably provided for workers in the mill. The mill was for grinding corn and had four acres of supporting ponds, formerly in front of the pub, which allowed for continuous operation.

The mill had a chequered history until it was demolished during the development of the South Metropolitan Gas Company which opened in 1887 on the northern part of the peninsula. It was biggest such site in the world and built to a revolutionary design. By 1902, the business was handling 1,200,000 tonnes of coal annually from the gas works jetty which was demolished for the Millennium Exhibition. The jetty is now the site of North Greenwich Pier with 'Quantum Cloud' by Anthony Gormley.

A local resident, who was a site manager for English Partnerships and an employee of the gas works, rescued a War Memorial which remembers the employees of the gas works, and today it stands near The Pilot Inn.

Access: West Parkside SE10 0BE
Opening times: Always open
Facilities: Benches, The Pilot Inn
Designation: Public Park, Metropolitan Open Land
Size: 3 hectares (7 acres)

Central Park in December

Greenwich
Peninsula
Ecology Park

Beautiful! Interesting! Fun!

This used to be the site of Redpath Brown's steel works from 1900–29, with the jetty for the steelworks now in the yacht club. Norton's Barge Yard was on the foreshore. In just twenty years, the Ecology Park has developed from an industrial site into a home for a surprisingly varied wildlife population.

And the birds, butterflies and insects have been attracted here because there are seven different habitats in the park.

A borehole feeds two lakes which are surrounded by marshland where reeds, flag irises, rushes, sedges and alders flourish. And a shingle beach is home to wasps. Grebes and warblers, amongst others, enjoy this habitat. Coppiced willows fill a small woodland on the edge of the park and help remove the pollutants in the soil.

In the centre of the park there is a small wildflower meadow where the wildflowers attract bees, butterflies and insects, which in turn sustain bats and frogs. Wildlife surveys have identified several rare species of moths, and well over 100 species of bees and other *Hymenoptera*, including over forty rare or threatened species and two species first found in the Ecology Park. The two bird hides allow observation of the wide variety of species which visit the park, including migratory birds which join the local population in their journeys north to south and back again every year. Local schools are welcomed and visits are closely tied to the school curriculum.

This wonderful small park is very important, not only because it gives us some understanding of the peninsula's landscape before it was industrialised, but also because it demonstrates the huge contribution which even a small space can make to biodiversity.

The site opened in 2002, ownership was transferred to The Land Trust in 2011, and now The Conservation Volunteers (TCV) manage the site with the help of volunteers.

Access: John Harrison Way SE10 0QZ
Opening times: Wednesday to Sunday, 10.00 am to 5.00 pm
Facilities: Classroom, exhibition centre, bird hides, café in Oval square, toilets, disabled access, waymarked walking route
Designation: SINC of Borough Importance Grade I, Urban Wetland, Green Flag Park
Size Ecology Park & Southern Park: 5 hectares (12 acres)
Greenwich Peninsula Ecology Park: gpep@tcv.org.uk

15

Red Admiral butterfly (top left), Tufted vetch (top left), and bull thistle (bottom right)

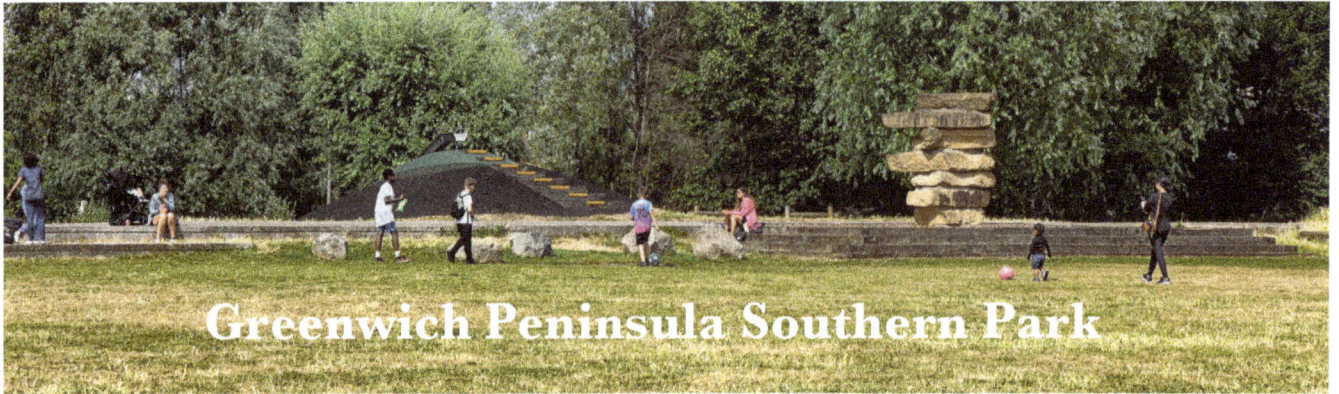

Greenwich Peninsula Southern Park

There are always people on the open expanse of grassland which is Southern Park. They may be strolling, playing games, or just sitting. A children's playground entertains squealing children, indigenous woodland is maturing on the perimeters and there are areas of wildflower plantings.

The Southern Park acts as a small village green for the surrounding blocks of flats and was acquired by The Land Trust in 2015.

Access: West Parkside SE10 0QQ
Opening times: Always open
Facilities: Children's playground, benches
Designation: SINC of Borouh Importance Grade I

16

Ballast Quay Gardens

Ballast Quay is a very old trading quay on the Thames. Cargo ships (sailing ships) needed ballast to stabilise them after they had unloaded, and they took this on at Ballast Quay. This might be gravel, chalk or sand, or even 'wet ballast' from dredging the river. Maze Hill Station now stands in one of these quarries and there were others between Blackheath and Greenwich. In 1800, Ballast Quay and Street were renamed Union Wharf but have now reverted.

In the 19th century, the coal trade from the north east was extremely important to London for domestic use, and to power the new trains and industrial development. The plethora of ships caused traffic jams in the Thames and so the Thames Conservancy (now the Environment Agency) built the Harbour Master's House at Union Wharf in 1855 to control the flow of traffic through the docks. This was one of several control points on the river. The post ended when the Port of London Authority took control of the river at the beginning of the 20th century, but the quay continued to be used by the neighbouring Lovell's Wharf.

By the mid–1960s, the wharf was derelict and that was when Hilary Peters, "a pilgrim without destination,"[15] persuaded Morden College to lease her the wharf and a house across the road. She made the garden, and her business, Union Wharf Nursery Garden, was the driving force behind the gardens at St Katherine's Docks and the Surrey Docks City Farm.

Today, the garden overlooking the Thames is a calm oasis which is cherished by Diane Greenwood with the help of GoodGym Greenwich, but Hilary Peters' spirit is still present.

Access: Ballast Quay SE10 9PD
The gardens are privately owned but open to the public on special, advertised occasions

17

The Harbour Master's House
seen from the garden

Diane Greenwood in the garden (below) and
GoodGym Greenwich lending a hand (left)

River Gardens

River Gardens are on the Thames Path between Ballast Quay and Enderby House in a section of the Greenwich Peninsula which had an important industrial history.

The Coles Child family business was coal, coke and cement, and it was based at Belvedere Wharf, near today's South Bank Centre. In 1836, William Coles Child (1817–73) wanted to expand the business and leased land (the Great Meadow and Dog Kennel Field) from the Trustees of Morden College. In the 1840s, this was Greenwich Wharf, which was developed for coal shipments and other industries.

He also built houses, and the names of Durham coalfields live on here in the Pelton Arms (a very pleasant and old–fashioned pub), and Whitworth, Graddyll and Caradoc Streets. Pelton Street was previously Willow Walk, which ran along the dyke guarding the south side of the marshes. When the coal business declined in the 1920s, this became Lovell's Wharf. Finally, gas production in London ended in 1970 and there was no more need of coal, or the colliers.

Enderby House was built in the 1840s by the Enderby family. They operated a rope and canvas business on the site and their whaling ships were heavily involved in the exploration and naming of Antarctica. Today it is a pub on the Thames and owned by Young & Co's Brewery.

Next to the pub, and alongside the river, is River Gardens, a housing development by Bellway, with pleasing landscaping between the blocks of flats and along the Thames Path. It is conveniently placed between the Cutty Sark pub and Enderby House — do wander along here!

Access: Pelton Road SE10 0NY leading to the Thames Path
Opening times: Always open

18

Christchurch School Community Garden

What a wonderfully surprising, friendly and natural site on the Greenwich Peninsula!

Christchurch School Community Garden was founded by Fiona Machen Harrison, Sheila Keeble and Patrick Ives in 2017 with the aim of providing a beautiful, tranquil, green space in a very urban community.

"We encourage community members of all ages to join us on our open days to learn about organically growing delicious, sustainable, zero air miles food, beautiful flowers, shrubs and trees. We also keep bees and produce delicious honey to sell to the community."[16]

The volunteers have planted a narrow line of hedging and wildflowers on the pavement — please can we have more of these pavement gardens!

The Community Garden stands on Blackwall Lane, formerly Marsh Lane and the old road into the marshes. It is attached to the school belonging to the Koinonia Federation, which has two schools occupying three campuses: St Mary Magdalene Woolwich, St Mary Magdalene Peninsula and Christ Church Primary School.

The garden was awarded 'Outstanding' in the 'It's Your Neighbourhood' category in London in Bloom 2024.

Access: 45 Comerell Street SE10 0DZ
Opening times: Fridays 10.30 am to 3.00 pm
Designation: Community Garden
Christchurch Community Garden: https://www.cscg.info

71

BLACKHEATH

'Blackheath' describes two things today: a vast, flat and open area of heathland but also an area of housing to the east, which is mainly the Cator Estate. And in the past the history of the eastern area overlapped with that of Kidbrooke and Charlton.

The Heath

The name, Blackheath, may be derived from Bleak Heath, or perhaps it was the colour of the soil? It was once covered in heather, gorse and acid grassland, but today only patches of the original cover remain, with indigenous plants appropriate to the acid grassland such as sheep's sorrel, hawkweed, storksbill, trefoils, vetches and clovers.

Blackheath is particularly attractive in the early summer when the roadsides are lined with colourful wildflowers, and the grass is treated as meadow and cut once or twice annually.

Under the grass lie the Blackheath Beds which were extensively quarried in the 18th and 19th centuries to supply London's building trade with gravel, sand, and chalk.

The two World Wars changed the appearance of the Heath.

Marr's Ravine, Crown Pits and Washerwomen's Pits were three quarries which were filled in with rubble after WWII. Eliot Pit, GLA 24, in the south west corner of the Heath, resembles a woodland today with mature trees and dense undergrowth. In the north east corner, Vanbrugh Pits, GLA 63, show the original appearance of the Heath with exposed Blackheath pebbles, and bright yellow gorse and broom in the spring. Oak, ash, birch and lime trees have also established here.

The Greenwich Natural History Club reported that in 1859 the Heath "still supported a wide variety of wildlife as well: brown hares, stoats, weasels, common lizards, natterjack toads and such birds of heath and common land as yellowhammers, corn buntings, linnets, redpolls, meadow pipits, tree pipits, nightingales, various warblers and grey partridges. Even the Dartford warbler was reported there in 1830."[17] A century and a half later it is a different story.

Four of the original seven ponds survive, but only Folly Pond, once the Real or Royal Pond, in the Crown Pits quarry, is in Greenwich.

And because of its proximity to the centre of London, the heath has a long history of notable events.

The Romans' Watling Street from Dover to London crossed the Heath, which was in following centuries the gathering place for rebellions and ceremonials. The Danish invaders camped here in 1011; the followers of Wat Tyler gathered on the Heath during the Peasants' Revolt in 1381; the Jack Cade rebels, opposing taxation, camped on the Heath in 1450; and the Cornishmen rebelled against taxation in 1497 and many were killed in a fight on the Heath.

Fairs are a regular feature of the Heath, and the wide expanses of grassland are also ideal for sport. The Royal Blackheath Golf Club (now based in Eltham) was established on the Heath in 1766, the first golf club outside Scotland, and is remembered in Goffers Road. Cricket was played on the Heath from the 18th century, and by 1890, the London County Council (LCC) was maintaining thirty–six pitches. The Blackheath Football Club was founded in 1862 and now shares a base with the Blackheath Cricket Club in Rectory Fields in Charlton. (The oldest clubs playing by Rugby Union rules are known as Football Clubs, which is somewhat confusing.) And these days, the Heath and Greenwich Park are the starting points for the London Marathon.

The area is manorial waste, poor quality open ground which cannot be used for horticultural or agricultural purposes or built on, but over time there have been encroachments. The major landowner is the Legge family, later the Earls of Dartmouth, who enclosed part of the Heath in the west and south east and sanctioned the building of some houses from the 17th century. Residential development around the perimeters of the Heath escalated in the 1800s, stimulated by the arrival of the railways in the mid–19th century.

The Crown owns the land north of the A2, while land to the south belongs to the Lord of the Manor, the Earl of Dartmouth. Today, Blackheath is managed by Greenwich and Lewisham Borough Councils.

Access: A2 Road, SE7 3BT
Opening times: Always open
Facilities: Seats, information boards
Designation: SINC of Metropolitan Importance,
Green Flag Public Open Space
Size of entire Heath: c.112 hectares (c.275 acres)
The Blackheath Society: www.blackheath.org

Essential reading:

All books by Neil Rhind (see bibliography)

Below: Vanbrugh Pits in Spring

Cator Estate

The Cator Estate has a long history as farmland and countryside; today's housing is quite a recent development.

The Domesday Book says Wricklemarsh was in the Hundred of Greenwich and it was held by Odo, the half–brother of William the Conqueror, but it probably reverted to the Crown after the rebellion of 1088 and Odo's banishment. It was perhaps an estate with a mansion house and farmlands rather than a manor, and fell across several parish boundaries. In the 16th century it was an agricultural hamlet with mainly arable land and pasturage, some woods, and heathland.

By 1669, most of the estate was owned by Sir John Morden. After his death, in 1723, Sir Gregory Page bought the estate, enclosed land and built Wricklemarsh House. The next owner was John Cator. From 1783 he owned c.110 hectares (c.275 acres) of parkland and agricultural land, demolished the mansion (he lived in Beckenham Place Park to which he transferred the façade of Wricklemarsh House) but continued the farmland. When his nephew inherited in the early 1800s, it was the start of residential development for the affluent, with spacious villas in large grounds, but progress was slow until the railways arrived in Blackheath.

In the 1950s, the Blackheath Cator Estate Residents bought the estate. The Span Housing Consortium was developed by Eric Lyons and Geoffrey Townsend, who wanted to build sympathetic housing in natural, landscaped surroundings. Developments were built between 1956 and 1980 and included The Priory, Corner Green, The Plantation, and Hallgate estates.

Pond Close Green SE3 0SH

Pond Road follows the line of the avenue which led from the Page's Wricklemarsh Mansion to an entrance gate on the Heath. Pond Close Green was a water basin which was an overflow pond for the Upper Kidbrook, and from here water was pumped to Wricklemarsh House. In the 1950s, the pond was filled in by the council.

Pond Close Green

Casterbridge Pond in the Brooklands Park Estate

Casterbridge Pond SE3 9AH

John Cator's nephew, also John Cator, gave £4,000 and land for a new church for local people when housing started to develop. The church opened in 1828 and was known as 'Mr Cator's Chapel.' (The builder was George Smith who lived in Brooklands House, now divided into flats.) The building was consecrated as the parish church of St Michael and All Angels in 1874 and is listed Grade II*.

Casterbridge was the Vicarage for St Michael's Church, a mansion set in a nineteen–acre estate laid out in meadows, and with a lake fed by the Middle Kidbrook.

The mansion was demolished in the 1950s to make way for the Brooklands Park Estate.

The developers, the LCC, were careful to preserve and protect the mature willow, oak and copper beech trees on the estate, and the ornamental lake. An original conduit house still stands on the edge of the lake.

On the island in the lake is a statue of 'Ganges', created by Raffaele Monti, which once stood in the grounds of the Crystal Palace in Sydenham. Another of Monti's statues for the Crystal Palace, 'Pacific', reclines in Dacres Road in Sydenham.

Morden College

What a wonderful place in which to retire! Homes here are set in glorious parkland, peaceful and quiet, with easy access to all the facilities for which you might wish.

Sir John Morden (1623–1708) was born in the City of London, apprenticed to his uncle, Sir William Soame, and joined the Levant (Turkey) Company. He was posted to Aleppo and eventually returned to London in 1659 with a substantial fortune.

In 1669, he bought the Manor of Wricklemarsh in Blackheath (for £4,200), a 250–acre estate, as a home for himself and his wife. Then, in 1695, he founded Morden College in the north east of the estate. His intention was to provide board, lodging and a pension for merchants of East India Company (EIC) or Levant Company status who had fallen on hard times.

The college was supported by acquisitions of land in the area. In 1698, Sir John Morden bought the East Greenwich Estate (Manor of Old Court) and its freehold from Lady Boreman, and he, and then his trustees, also acquired land on the west and south sides of the heath.

Under the terms of his will, college trustees were drawn sequentially from the Levant Company, EIC, or from the Aldermen of the City of London, who have provided the charity's trustees since 1884.

Morden College has expanded considerably since the 17th century, and today the College provides accommodation for its residents in both Blackheath and Ralph Perring Court in Beckenham, which more than doubled the capacity of the College in 1991.

Access: St Germans Place SE3 0PW
Opening times: Selected Open Days
Size: 6 hectares (14 acres)
Morden College: https://mordencollege.org.uk

KIDBROOKE

"It was anciently written Cicebroc," says Hasted,[18] meaning 'the brook where the kites were seen,' and 'broc' suggests marshy land in old English. The land slopes downwards from Shooters Hill, and the Quaggy, the Lower Kidbrook, Middle Kidbrook and the Upper Kidbrook all flow through the area to drain into the Ravensbourne at Confluence Park in Lewisham, so the name is apt.

The history of Kidbrooke is tricky to unravel! In the Rochester Text of the early 12th century, Kidbrooke is the chapel-of-ease for Charlton Parish Church. The Countess of Hereford probably owned Wricklemarsh as well as Kidbrooke at the time and bequeathed her lands in Kidbrooke to the Monastery of St Mary Overie in Southwark.

A mediaeval church stood between Brook Lane and Delme Crescent, but by 1428 there was no priest and most of the population seems to have disappeared. (Was this a consequence of The Black Death?) Until the Church of St James was built in 1867, Kidbrooke continued as a Liberty, or extraparochial hamlet, and the parishioners used the church in Charlton.

The Manor of Kidbrooke returned to the Crown at the Dissolution of the Monasteries. King James I granted it to Sir William Garway from whom it passed to his son-in-law, Edward Blount of Wricklemarsh, and subsequently a number of different owners. It was last sold in 1717 to the Cragg family, and the Earl of St Germans remains the Lord of the Manor with some manorial rights.

In the mid-19th century, Kidbrooke was still in Kent and covered 750 acres of countryside, farmland or woodland. It stretched from the Royal Herbert Hospital to St Germans Place, down to Lee Road where the boundary was the Quaggy, along the Lower Kidbrook, and back to today's intersection of Well Hall Road and Shooters Hill Road. Curiously, a narrow stretch of land from Shooters Hill towards Morden College and Blackheath Village belonged in Charlton and divided the parish.

James Thorne could write in 1876, "from Kidbrooke new church there are pleasant field paths to Eltham ... with the roof of the great hall of Eltham Palace as landmark the whole way."[19] Even in 1912, Sir Walter Besant wrote of open fields and market gardens between Hervey Road and Eltham Road.

There were three big farms, but they were sometimes subdivided and confusingly their names varied as well:
- Kidbrooke Farm included Hither Farm (also known as Upper Farm), Middle Kidbrooke Farm and Hill Farm. Later all three were known as Manor Farm.
- Lower Kidbrooke Farm (also known as Kidbrooke Green Farm and Stud Farm) was partly in Kidbrooke and partly in Eltham. In the 20th century this farm had an orchard known as Chandlers Orchard; today's Birdbrook Nature Reserve was on the farm.
- The southern part of the Wricklemarsh Estate was farmed by William Morris, a farmer with big holdings in Lee and Eltham as well.

An auction notice of 1810 from the area listed livestock including horses, cows, sheep (meat and wool), pigs and poultry, and crops of hay, barley, oats, potatoes and fruit. In the 1920s, draught horses took grain from these farms to Whitbread's Brewery in Chiswell Street in the City, and Express Dairies only stopped farming here in 1937. (Milk, a perishable product, was still produced locally at this time.)

Change started in the early 19th century, increased with the advent of the railways, and continued into the 20th century as new roads were built. Even so, it was only in the 1930s that the major changes happened.

In 1917, a Royal Air Corps storage and maintenance depot was set up on both sides of the railway line at Kidbrooke Station and a year later it became RAF Kidbrooke. A prisoner of war camp was built on the site of today's Thomas Tallis School.

The site expanded in 1938 when the government bought Kidbrooke Green and Lower Kidbrooke Farm buildings nearby for a barrage balloon depot, to protect London from low-flying aircraft. During its years in service, RAF Kidbrooke also provided glider training, language training and training for military transport. The station finally closed

Kidbrooke Village from Sutcliffe Park

in 1965. Some of the buildings are now storage for the National Maritime Museum, next to the new Prince Philip Maritime Collections Centre.

At this point, the government released land for the Ferrier Estate which was completed in 1972. It was social housing in the brutalist style, built in grey concrete, and separated in appearance and population from its surroundings. This seemed to encourage high levels of crime. In 2004, the government approved full–scale redevelopment of the area. Tenants were moved out, the buildings demolished and Berkeley Homes and Southern Housing started on the construction of the new Kidbrooke Village.

"Social sustainability combines design of the physical environment with a focus on how the people who live in and use a space relate to each other and function as a community. It is enhanced by development, which provides the right infrastructure to support a strong social and cultural life, opportunities for people to get involved, and scope for the place and the community to evolve." This is what Berkeley Homes promotes as their ethos.[20]

These are not new ideas.

Sir Ebenezer Howard was describing Garden City ideals at the end of the 19th century, and Jane Jacobs wrote of 'placemaking' in the 1960s.

The result is a beautiful and varied urban neighbourhood with a mixed population, which recognises the importance of wildlife and nature and includes them in people's residential environment to enhance physical and mental well–being. Today it is hard to imagine the rural Kidbrooke of less than a century ago.

Essential reading:

Egan, Michael, *Kidbrooke: Eight Hundred Years of a Farming Community*, (1983, Greenwich and Lewisham Antiquarian Society)

Egan, Michael, *Wricklemarsh Revisited*, (2017, Kent ArchaeologicalSociety)

Rhind, Neil, *Blackheath Village & Environs*, Vol 2, (1983, Blackheath Bookshop Ltd)

Birdbrook Nature Reserve

This was once on Lower Kidbrooke Farm. By 1982, British Telecom owned the site and gave the London Wildlife Trust a licence to manage it as a nature reserve. The Rochester Way relief road was a threat in the mid–1990s, but volunteers from the trust lobbied the government and the site was saved.

The delightful Birdbrook Nature Reserve is heavily treed, with some scrubland and grassland, and lots of wildflowers, but there are also ponds. It is one of the most important sites in London for newts, as well as many other insects and a wide variety of birds.

Birdbrook Road Nature Reserve SE3 9QP, is open by appointment only
It is a SINC of Metropolitan Importance
Size: 1.1 hectare (2.7 acres)

Below: *Birdbrook Nature Reserve, with perennial sweetpea and purple crown vetch*

Birdbrook Road & Carnbrook Road Parks

Two delightful park/playgrounds have recently been made in this area.

Birdbrook Road park is a pretty open space with some pieces of play equipment in a ring of wildflowers.

Carnbrook Road Park is always crowded with local residents and happy children. The park is alongside the Rochester Way and imaginatively landscaped with undulating perimeters, new trees, and masses of wildflowers in the summer.

This park was possibly orchards in Lower Kidbrooke Farm in the 19th century, and in the area of the Lower Kidbrook stream. It is a most attractive children's park and playground and will become more so as the years pass and the trees develop.

Opposite above: Birdbrook Road Park SE3 9QB
Below: Carnbrook Road Park SE3 8AG

24

Tracy's Garden on Birdbrook Road

Will Crooks Gardens

Will Crooks Gardens is a narrow strip of grass, trees and hedging on an embankment just north of the A2 and close to the Birdbrook Nature Reserve. Like the nature reserve, it was farmland until the 1930s.

Small leaf lime trees, rowan trees, birches, horse chestnuts and hazels line the path and frame the view towards Kidbrooke Village. Although it is noisy and often littered, this hidden short walk is surprisingly attractive.

Will Crooks (1852–1921) was a remarkable man. He was born into extreme poverty in Poplar, East London. His father was disabled, and although Mrs Crooks was illiterate she managed to scrape together enough money as a seamstress to support the family. Somehow she found a penny a week to send William to school. He was intelligent and hardworking and rose from an apprenticeship at the age of fourteen to be the Labour MP for Woolwich in 1901. During his working life, he achieved the reform of workhouses, and fair wages and pensions for the elderly working class. He was unafraid of speaking his mind. It was his view that Parliament, which was created by the people, should be at the service of the people and all the people, instead of at the service of the powerful and the wealthy.

In his final speech on the Unemployed Bill in 1905 "Crooks argued that even the loafer would become a better man by being given, not the charity that demoralised, but a day's work for a day's pay."[21] Perhaps we could have found a more generous way of remembering him?

Access: Birdbrook Road SE9 6JD
Opening times: Always open
Designation: Amenity Green Space
Size: 1.12 hectares (2.47 acres)

Kidbrooke Green Park & Nature Reserve

When Kidbrooke's mediaeval village disappeared in the 14th century, the land returned to countryside, although maps indicate that Kidbrooke Green remained as a green, and common land. Lower Kidbrooke Farm lay in this area.

In 1938, the government bought the green and farm buildings to extend RAF Kidbrooke with a barrage balloon site. Part of the green became allotments in 'Dig for Victory' during WWII. When the station closed in the 1960s, the land was transferred to the council for housing, and the park may date from that time.

The nature reserve dates from the 1980s when the Rochester Way relief road was built. Like the park, the reserve is on heavy, damp, clay soil and has a number of small ponds which are home to newts, including great crested newts, a European protected species. The council is working with Froglife charity to improve this habitat.

Kidbrooke Green Park was initially known as the Rochester Way Playing Fields but renamed in 2003. It is a pleasant, grassed area with recreational facilities and an avenue of mature trees alongside the nature reserve. A hidden path between the park and the A2 connects to Kidbrooke Village, Cator Parks and Sutcliffe Park, and forms an interesting circular walk.

Access: Nelson Mandela Way SE3 9QR
Opening times: Park always open; Nature Reserve closed
Facilities: Outdoor gym gear, tennis courts, multipurpose game court, benches
Designation: Public Open Land, Nature Reserve is SINC of Metropolitan Importance
Size: 3.2 hectares (8 acres)
Friends of Kidbrooke Green Park:
friendsofkidbrookegreenpark@yahoo.co.uk

Below: *Enjoying the open green space in November*

Above: *On the hidden path between the park and the A2*
Below: *Outdoor gym in Kidbrooke Green Park*

Cator Parks in Kidbrooke Village

The Mediaeval village vanished without trace, but now there is a new Kidbrooke Village, developed by Berkeley Homes working with HTA Design and the London Wildlife Trust. And it has new parks — Cator Parks (North and South).

Kidbrooke Village is a community of varied ages living in flats and terraced housing, with offices, shops, a children's nursery and a train station. As well as individual gardens, there are landscaped public squares and streets, and podium landscapes — gardens above ground level, usually for residents only, and often built over a car park. The development was Highly Commended in the Placemaking category of the New London Awards 2020, and Cator Park won the Sir David Attenborough Award for Enhancing Biodiversity in the same year.

"The thinking that went into Cator Park started more than twenty years ago, with the formation of our landscape discipline. Our design approach has evolved during this time, changing in emphasis from the creation of formal and hard landscapes to a focus on bringing people and nature closer together, by creating softer, biodiverse spaces as typified by Cator Park."[22]

A new chalk stream flows quietly in Cator Park North, while Cator Park South has a large lake. SuDS (sustainable drainage systems) mimic natural drainage of water and reduce the amount of water entering the sewage system, which is reaching capacity in London. Rainwater is redirected into the ponds, lake and the sunken wet areas which also attract water birds and herons. The meadows are planted with wildflowers favoured by birds, butterflies, bees and other insects, and a young grove of trees in Cator Park North will one day be a little woodland.

The delightful, open, and varied children's play area is made from recycled materials and quite unlike the standard children's playground.

Cator parks are managed by Berkeley Homes as beautiful and interesting green spaces which will mature over time and in which you can relax and be part of nature.

Left:
Wild teasel
Common yarrow
Purple loosestrife
Common toad flax
Opposite:
The lake in Cator Park South

Access: Kidbrooke Park Road SE3 9FW
Opening times: Always open
Facilities: Benches, children's playground, multipurpose ball court
Designation: Private Parks open to the public
Size: 8 hectares (20 acres)

28

Both pages: *Views in Cator Park North in Autumn and Summer*

Sutcliffe Park

29

Sutcliffe Park is surely one of the most spectacular small parks in South East London. In its centre, the lake and wetlands are planted with rushes, willows and alders, and are rich in wildlife. Herons, little egrets, kingfishers, Egyptian and Canada geese, mallards, coots, and reed warblers crowd the water, which is patrolled by a majestic Bonnie, the swan. Her mate Clyde died a few years ago, and the Friends keep close watch over Bonnie — could they find her a mate?

Trees in the park are plentiful, with an avenue of horse chestnut trees along Kidbrooke Park Road and another mixed avenue on the east side of the park. And most of the grass is treated as meadow.

The site was originally Harrow Meadow, and it was marshy ground through which the River Quaggy meandered. In 1873, Harrow Cottages stood roughly where Eltham Road and Kidbrooke Park Road meet at the traffic lights today.

In the 1930s, the Woolwich Borough Council built housing in the area and set aside thirty–five acres for a park which was laid out as playing fields, with the river buried underground. The park opened in 1937 and was named after Mr John Sutcliffe, a former engineer in the Royal Borough of Greenwich. The athletics track was added in 1954.

The Quaggy and the Ravensbourne rivers have a history of flooding and in the past were culverted to take the water out of area as quickly as possible. By the 1990s, the thinking had changed. The Quaggy Waterways Action Group (QWAG) campaigned to restore rivers to their natural course, with small flood plains upstream to slow down the flow of water.

Sutcliffe Park was radically re–landscaped in 2003 by the Environment Agency. The central area was lowered to create a flood plain, and the river returned to its meandering course through the meadow. The wetland area was designated a Local Nature Reserve in 2006 and received the Living Wetlands Award in 2007.

The park offers good exercise opportunities. The athletics track, home to the famous Cambridge Harriers Athletics Club, has been refurbished and is now one of the best tracks in south London. The perimeter path is 0.9 miles (2,000 steps), the Sutcliffe Park Sports Centre offers various activities, and there is also outdoor gym gear and a children's playground.

Access: Eltham Road SE9 5LW
Opening times: 9.00 am to dusk
Facilities: Athletics track run by GLL, outdoor table tennis, outdoor gym gear, children's playground, benches
Designation: Nature reserve is SINC of Borough Importance Grade II, Green Flag Public Park
Size: 14.2 hectares (35 acres)
Friends of Sutcliffe Park: https: www.facebook.com

The mixed avenue of trees on the east side of Sutcliffe Park

Bonnie cruising in the lake and (below) the Quaggy spreading on to its flood plain after heavy rains

The meadows in Sutcliffe Park on a stormy day, and a member of Thames21 explaining river management to volunteers from BNP Paribas

Quaggy Playing Fields & Nature Trail

There are two important issues here: the preservation of sports fields in an increasingly densely populated area and the development of a nature trail. This important project has strong support from CPRE: "The Quaggy Playing Fields are a classic example of 'land banking' where individuals and developers buy land and sit on it in the hope that they could wear down the council into overturning the land designation and allowing development."[23]

Around the River Quaggy between Kidbrooke, Lee Green, and Blackheath, lies a set of playing fields which together form a unique and vital sporting destination and green 'lung' for the immediate and wider areas. Twenty years ago, fourteen fields were all actively used by sports clubs. Today, five have been developed for housing and a further four are under threat, including the Willow Country Club and Manor Way grounds.

Since buying these last two grounds, supposedly protected as Metropolitan Open Land, (MOL),[24] the owner has closed off access and the sites have deteriorated. However, the RBG Playing Pitch Strategy for 2015–28 has identified that restoration of these sites would contribute to meeting demand in the borough.

Local people and sports clubs want to create a new River Quaggy Sports Park, "a coherent park with a distinct identity where members of local communities and beyond can enjoy the benefits of well–managed sports fields and more generally as an open access site for recreation, walking, leisure and nature."[25] One remaining field on Weigall Road is used by London Legends FC, which was set up in 2018 and caters for children, men and women. Coaches and staff members are all FA qualified.

The second project is to develop a trail along the River Quaggy which links Sutcliffe Park to Lee Green. It is an exciting opportunity to create a beautiful and beneficial little nature reserve. The trail could include small flood plains, as this is an area of high flood risk, and this will encourage biodiversity in both plants and wildlife of various kinds, similar to what has been achieved in Sutcliffe Park and further away in Chinbrook Meadows.

Let's hope borough councils and land owners will be able to collaborate generously for the benefit of the local communities.

Access: Weigall Road SE12 8HG
Lee Forum: www.leeforum.org.uk

30

Above: Proposed plan for the area, and *Below:* The River Quaggy flowing under the Weigall Road Bridge

CHARLTON

The Domesday Book of 1086 tells us that "William FitzOgier holds Charlton of the bishop. It is assessed at 1 sulung [240 acres]... Godwine and Alweard held this land of the king as 2 manors." Charlton was known as Ceorltun or Cerletone in old English, meaning 'farmstead of freemen or peasants.'

Charlton lies between Greenwich and Woolwich and is on two levels: an upland plateau with deep ravines or coombes down the hillside to the Woolwich Road, and the former marshes along the Thames. The village was on the upland plateau, centred round Charlton House (the former manor house) and its stables, St Nicholas Church and The Bugle Horn pub. St Luke's almshouses of the 18th century are nearby in Fairfield Grove.

Sir Adam Newton, tutor to Henry, Prince of Wales, a son of James I, bought the Manor of Charlton in 1607 and built Charlton House between 1607 and 1612, the only important Jacobean home still standing in London. It is believed the architect was Inigo Jones, who probably designed the summer house of c.1630 as well. Both buildings are Grade I listed. The manor stood in the Kent countryside and included farmland, woods and quarries. (Inigo Jones lived nearby in Cherry Orchard House.)

From 1767–1925 the Maryon–Wilson family were the Lords of the Manor. In WWI, the house was used as a military hospital, and in 1925, Sir Spencer Maryon–Wilson sold the house to the council and it was converted to a Community Centre after WWII.

In centuries past, the Thames regularly flooded the Charlton marshes. William Lambarde built an embankment in 1555 (today's Lombard's Wall) to protect his property and a river wall of the 16th century maintained the Charlton Level for grazing and farming. Even in 1912, there were sizable market gardens here.

The Manways were causeways across the marshes and toll roads. They remain today as Barrier Park (Hardens Manway), Penhall Road (Middle Manway) and Anchor and Hope Lane

The Bugle Horn pub in Charlton

Charlton Riverside - Angerstein Wharf

(Great Manway). Anchor and Hope Lane is the oldest route, and leads to a pub of the same name on the riverside, established in the 16th century, and owned by the Lord of the Manor.

Until the mid–1800s, countryside life prevailed; it was the new railways which brought change and industrial development. Some housing appeared in Eastcombe in the late 1800s, but most of the housing dates from the 20th century.

Ayles Ropeworks and Tar Kettleshop, which continued in the family until 1908, were amongst the first industries on the riverside, and by the 1930s, industry was thriving here.

Henry Castle and Sons, Shipbreakers, operated here from 1860 to the 1930s, and Libertys Department Store was a customer for their reclaimed timber. William Cory and Sons dates from 1838 and ran lighters which unloaded coal from the large colliers. By the 1870s they were handling more than half the seacoal in London. The company continues on the site, repairing and maintaining barges which transport waste out of central London. Atlas and Derrick Gardens was built for their employees c.1908.

British Ropes of 1912 made wire ropes for the Mulberry Harbours in WWII. The company, renamed Bridon, only closed in 1995. Siemens Brothers Telegraph and Telephone Works was the major business here 1860–1967. Their

buildings remain, next to the Thames Barrier. Glass bottles were manufactured behind the Anchor & Hope pub, using sand quarried in Charlton until 1920. United Glass Bottles made 4 million blood transfusion bottles, and London's entire milk bottle supply during WWII. The site was replaced in the 1960s by a Sainsbury distribution centre.

Starting in March 2023, the industrial area is being transformed into Charlton Riverside with up to 7,000 new homes and new jobs. While green spaces are planned, will they materialise? And the old buildings? "The surviving buildings tell stories that are variously of local, national, and — particularly pertaining to the telecommunications and wartime narratives — international significance."[26]

Redevelopment will be difficult, so will historical information be respected? Or will this be another development where the past is regarded as irrelevant and there are no open green spaces?

Essential reading:

Hounsell, Peter, *Bricks of Victorian London*, (2022, University of Hertfordshire Press, Studies in Regional and Local History, Vol.22)
Mills, Mary, *Greenwich and Woolwich at Work*, (2002, Sutton Publishing)
Smith, John G, *History of Charlton, Vols 1–3*, (1970-87, privately published)

Barrier Park

The Thames has always flooded its banks, but it took until 1954 before a technological solution was sought to provide protection to people and buildings.

The Thames Barrier is the world's largest movable flood barrier, and it was put in place between 1972 and 1982. The site was chosen because the river banks here are relatively straight and the chalk bed of the river is strong enough to support the structures.

The award–winning design was designed by Rendel, Palmer and Turner. The barrier protects Central London from tidal surges and flooding.

Barrier Park is a narrow park between the Thames Barrier and Woolwich main road and it is built on an ancient causeway over the marshes, Hardens Manorway, also known as Ardens Manway. Was it built by or named for S Hardin, a local farmer, in the 18th century? Today it carries the Green Chain Walk and Capital Ring Path.

The park offers a charming green space in rather bleak and rundown industrial surroundings where redevelopment is starting. There is a small pond in the north and meandering paths wind through a variety of indigenous trees and shrubs, and perennials.

As always, when you walk into a garden the atmosphere changes — do amble through this little park if you visit the Thames Barrier.

Access: Eastmoor Street SE7 8LX
Opening times: Always open
Facilities: None
Designation: SINC of Local Importance Grade II, Metropolitan Open Land
Size: 1.8 hectares (4.6 acres)

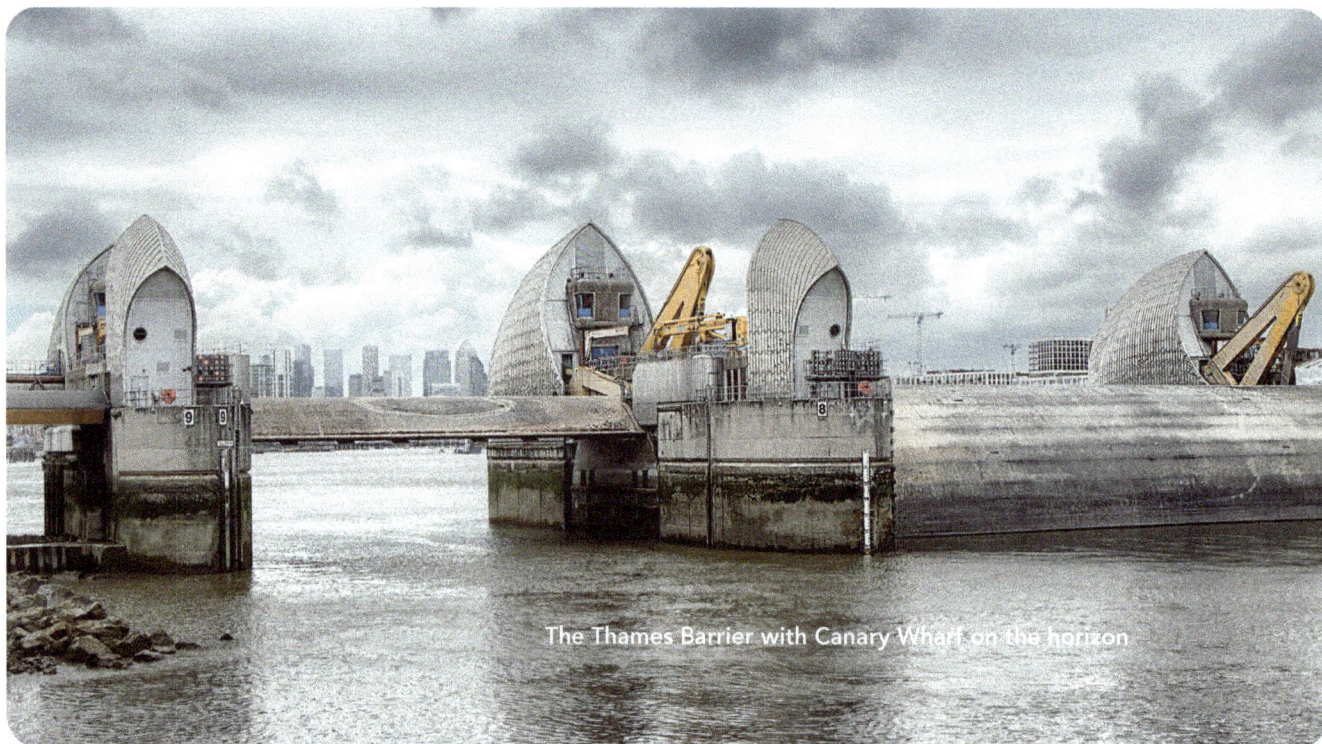

31

The Thames Barrier with Canary Wharf on the horizon

Barrier Park in autumn (above) and summer (below)

Charlton Cemetery

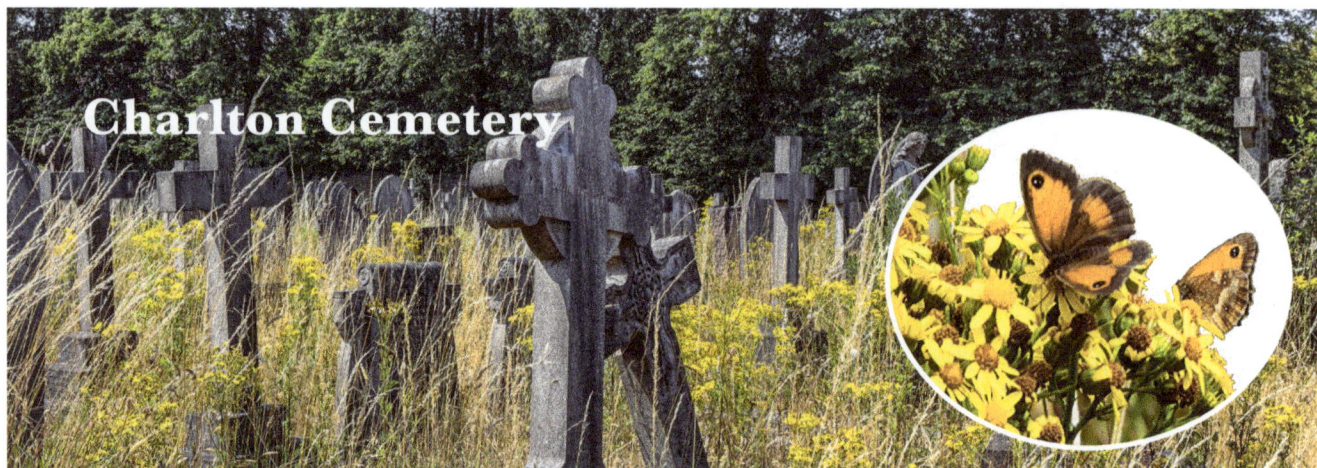

The original Victorian cemetery, with curving paths around the two chapels, is peaceful and calm. Time seems to stop under the old holm oaks and yew trees where the gravestones are gathered under the old holm oak and yew trees, some leaning over, unregimented and random like life itself.

The northern, older part of the cemetery is a conservation area where the council cut the grass once a year. Wildflowers such as mauve knapweed, yellow lady's bedstraw and common ragwort, amongst others, thrive and support clouds of butterflies and happy bees. Tall trees line the boundary. It feels like a country graveyard and is particularly attractive in spring and summer. The south side of the cemetery alongside Charlton Park Lane is somewhat bleaker.

Sir Thomas Maryon–Wilson, 8th Bart, sold five acres of his estate for £2,600 to the Greenwich Burial Board in 1854 for a new cemetery where "tasteful planting of trees and shrubs, careful gardening, and constant attention, have preserved and enhanced its superlative character."[27] This was one of the earliest cemeteries laid out under the new Burial Act. In 1890, the Board bought a further three acres from Sir John Maryon–Wilson, 9th Bart, for £3,000. And a final seven acres were added to the cemetery in the 20th century. Members of the family are buried here.

Charlton Cemetery has two 19th century chapels — one Anglican, the other non–conformist — which are Grade II listed. In 1866, a mortuary (now demolished) was added to hold the bodies of people drowned in the Thames and washed up in Charlton.

A War Memorial stands near the entrance, and there are 114 CWGC graves scattered throughout the cemetery, sometimes together with family members, which is always a sad sight.

Amongst the many service people buried here, a very modest tomb remembers Admiral Sir Watkin Owen Pell (1788–1869) who entered the RN in 1799 and lost his left leg in 1800 while serving on the Loire during the capture of the French frigate, Pallas. He was knighted in 1837 after an active and successful career.

As one might expect in a Victorian cemetery, there are several interesting tombs: Sir Geoffrey Callender was the first director of the National Maritime Museum; Jemima Ayley (1825–49) has an ornate tomb over a twenty–two–foot vault which includes the table and chairs used by her mourning relatives, apparently, and Thomas Murphy (d.1932), owner of Charlton Greyhound Race Track, has an imposing memorial with two greyhounds.

Access: Cemetery Lane SE7 8DZ
Opening times: Check the RBG website
Facilities: Benches, toilets
Designation: SINC of Borough Importance Grade II
Size: 6 hectares (15 acres)

Charlton House Gardens & Charlton Park

33

The gardens at Charlton House reflect how thinking about gardens has changed over time.

Charlton House was built by Sir Adam Newton, and the gardens must have been laid out at the same time, c.1612–1607, probably in the style of Tudor gardens. At this time, Salomon De Caus was working in the Royal palaces. He, and then Inigo Jones, introduced grottos, statuary, and water features into formal gardens. Sir Adam tutored a son of James I and so must have been aware of the work of de Caus — were these once garden features?

Sir Adam imported trees from the Mediterranean and his son, Sir Henry, was also a keen gardener. The black mulberry of 1649 was amongst the first in England and Lady Newton supplied cuttings of cherry laurels, which had only come to England in the late 16th century, to John Evelyn.

John Rocque's map of 1746 shows a formal layout with simple, symmetrical parterres on the north, east and south sides of the house, and avenues of trees. This accorded with the Italian and French styles which aimed to reflect the status of the owner, order and reason, rather than display plants.

During the long 18th century there was a change from formal designs to more natural landscapes which evoked emotions — enter 'Capability' Brown and others.

By 1784, Thomas Reynolds' map shows formal, symmetrical parterres in the walled garden, but on the north, curves have replaced straight lines in the parterre. Parterres on the east have gone, and the axial avenue of trees has been shortened. In 1797, Hasted noted, "Before the courtyard there is a long row of Cypress trees [Yew trees];"[28] a few of the trees still remain on the east front of the house.

In 1829, Sir Thomas Maryon–Wilson, 8th Bart, enclosed the village green, forming the sweeping driveway and front lawn, and a ha–ha of 1847 segregated the "splendid herd of deer,"[29] creating an uninterrupted vista towards Hanging Woods. He was a renowned botanist and loved hardy plants (perennials?) and shrubs like rhododendrons. Hypericum calcinum covered bare ground under large trees. Foxgloves were abundant, and plants included phlox, fuchsias, monkshood, statice, gaillardia grandiflora, penstemon, and pinks. The kitchen garden produced apples, pears and soft fruits, and the greenhouse allowed the cultivation of tender exotic plants and flowers for the house, as well as grapes.

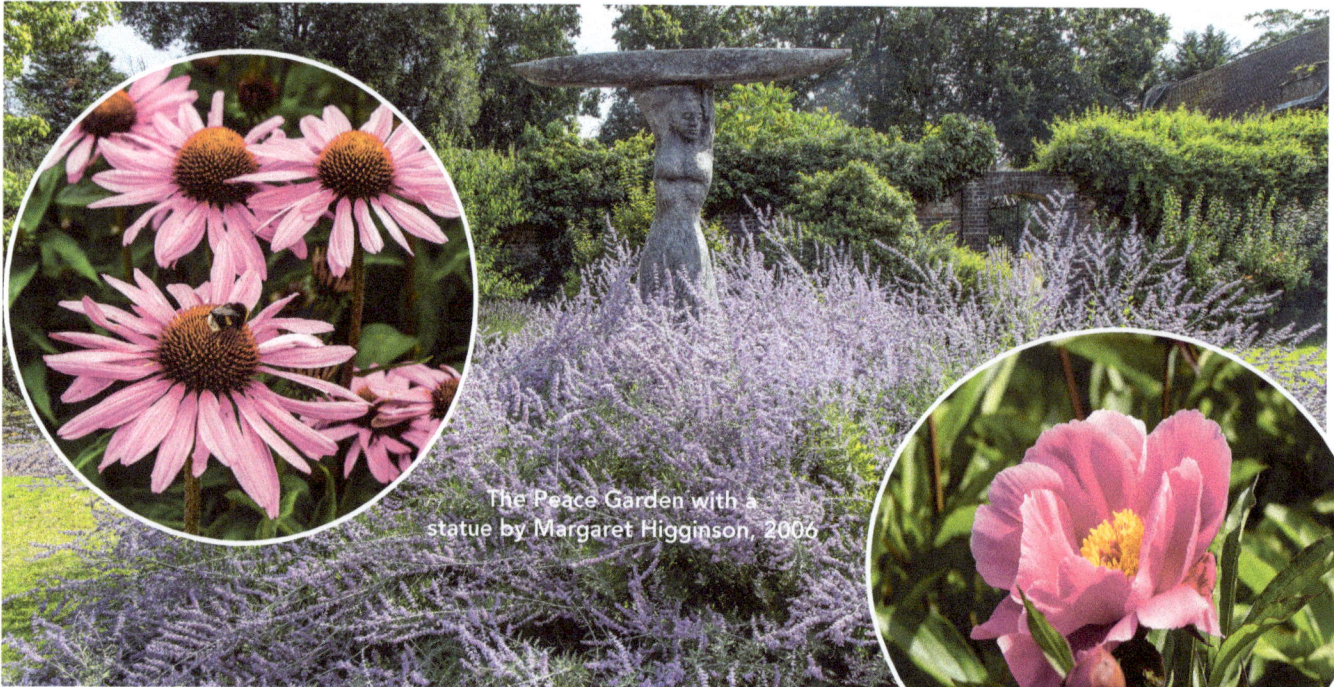

The Peace Garden with a statue by Margaret Higginson, 2006

Today concerns over climate change, loss of biodiversity, and limited resources mean the garden is changing again. The Head Gardener and enthusiastic volunteers have transformed two of the remaining three walled gardens into a colourful feast for pollinators, which respects the structure of the soil and the special characteristics of each of the seasons. Foliage colour and shape contrasts are key, as is low maintenance, so there is a no–dig policy and the plants create their own mulch. The gardeners were rewarded with the Judges Award for Volunteers and a Gold Medal in London in Bloom 2024.

Charlton Park offers several sports fields, and the Friends have sown a wildflower meadow on the old cricket pitch along Cemetery Lane.

Summerhouse by Inigo Jones and old mulberry tree

Access: Charlton Road SE7 8RE
Opening times: Check the website for garden opening times
Facilities: Two cafés, benches, sports fields, children's playground
Designation: Green Flag Public Park of 21 hectares (52 acres)
Charlton & Blackheath Amateur Horticultural Society (garden volunteers): www.cabahs.com

Nepalese Community Soccer Festival in Charlton Park

Market Day at Charlton House

Hornfair Park

34

In 1920, Stonefield Farm stood on Charlton Manor land, to the south of Charlton House, surrounded by orchards and fields. The LCC bought some of this land from the Maryon–Wilson family in 1926. It was intended for housing but an area proved surplus to requirement and was instead landscaped as a park and recreational grounds. Charlton Playing Fields opened in 1936 followed by Charlton Lido three years later.

The park was renamed Hornfair Park in 1948 in memory of Horn Fair.

In 1268, Henry III granted a three–day fair to Bermondsey Abbey, which owned Charlton Manor at that time. Could this have been the origin of Horn Fair? The annual Horn Fair was on the 18th October on the village green in front of Charlton House until this was enclosed in 1829. The fair then transferred to Fair Field (between Charlton Lane and Fairfield Grove) until it was suppressed in the late 19th century because of riotous behaviour. Today's Horn Fair in the grounds of Charlton House is a very tame affair by comparison!

Hornfair Park still has the original good recreational facilities (apart from the bowling green and pavilion) but it looks 'tired' and offers a challenging opportunity to the newly formed and enthusiastic Friends of Hornfair Park.

The Friends have ambitious plans to develop the park into a cherished community asset for local residents, families and visitors.

They plan an ecology survey to provide a baseline assessment of the park and identify opportunities to improve biodiversity. A new planting plan, appropriate to climate change and current resources, will be developed with the council's Parks and Open Spaces team, and they want to improve the park facilities working with local people to identify priorities. Most ambitiously the Friends would like to build a community hub which offers training, social and artistic opportunities, a welcoming and safe space for all, and an attached community café offering good value and locally sourced food. Perhaps there will even be homemade cakes? Irresistible!

Wow! Watch this space

Access: Shooters Hill Road SE18 4LX
Opening times: Always open
Facilities: Lido & gym (charge), children's paddling pool, basketball court, hard tennis courts, BMX track, football pitches, children's playground, café in the leisure centre
Designation: Public Park
Size: 10 hectares (25 acres)
Friends of Hornfair Park: www.facebook.com

Sunken garden

Sports field with wildflower meadow

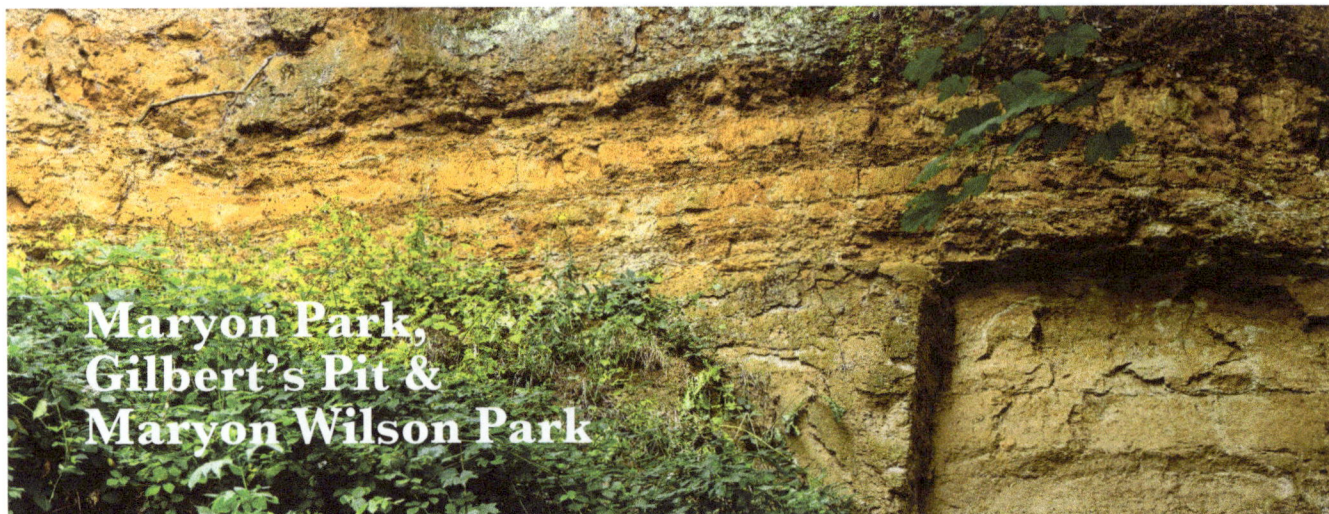

Maryon Park, Gilbert's Pit & Maryon Wilson Park

35

Be warned — these parks are seriously hilly! If you really want to explore, you will be going up and down, and up and down! But on a clear day there are wonderful views over London from Cox's Mount in Maryon Park, particularly when the trees are not yet in leaf.

The parks were once Hanging Wood in the Manor of Charlton, stretching from Charlton to Woolwich Common. They were a haunt for highwaymen but 'hanging' refers to the position on a steep hillside rather than a place of execution.

Sir Spencer Maryon–Wilson donated land to the LCC for a new park, which he opened to the public on 25 October 1890. The park was laid out by Lt Col J J Sexby, who talks of tennis courts, and a bandstand which provided a weekly concert in 'the season'. Just twenty years later, Sir Walter Besant wrote of "the beautiful Maryon Park [where] the pit has been completely metamorphised by skilful gardening, and the natural ruggedness has been carefully kept and brought into contrast with flower–beds and lawns."[30] In 1924, the Maryon Wilson family donated a further thirty–two acres of land in Hanging Woods to the LCC, and Maryon–Wilson Park opened two years later.

Today, the Green Chain Walk and Capital Ring cross both parks

Maryon Park & Gilbert's Pit

From the 18th century, the land here was quarried for sand, gravel and chalk in two adjoining pits which explains the park's strange, hollowed–out appearance.

Gilbert's Pit is a SSSI because the different geological layers, dating back 55 million years, are clearly exposed in the pit. It was mainly quarried for sand, and quarrying here only ended in 1938. It is sobering to realise that fifty–five million years of resources have vanished and can never be replaced. (The ridge path overlooking the Pit is not usually open to the public because it is dangerous, and the Pit is not part of the park.)

The lowest level of the Thanet sands was used for brass casting when molten metal was poured into a sand mould shaped from a wooded pattern. The next layer of mild loam was used for iron casting and the white sand above was used to make amber–coloured glass. Sand was also used as a cleaning agent from the 16th century, particularly in the kitchen where it absorbed grease from the kitchen fire, and in rooms which had a lot of outdoor traffic. Sometimes it was added to bricks.

On the western side of Maryon Park is a high ridge overlooking Gilbert's Pit. A Romano–British settlement stood here until c.400 AD.

Looking down into Gilbert's Pit, next to Maryon Park, in early April

Maryon Park

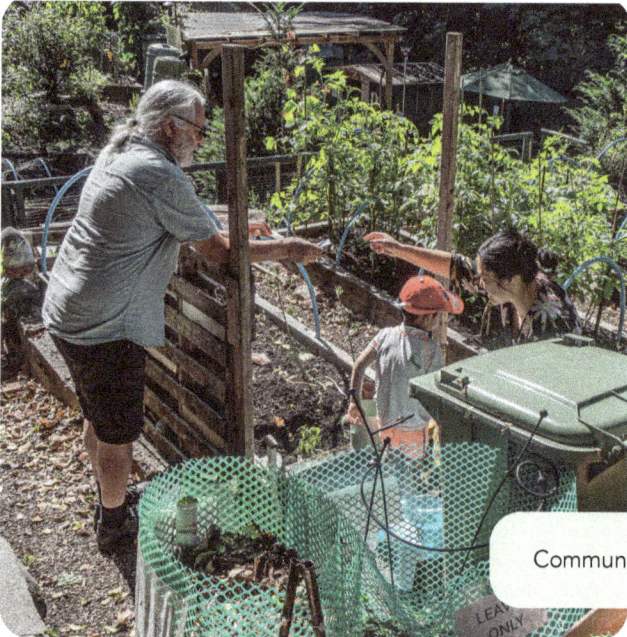

Community Garden

Cox's Mount overlooks the eastern part of the park and a semaphore station stood here in the 19th century, linked to Shooters Hill. It takes its name from Mr Cox of no.5 Charlton Terrace who rented the Mount from 1838 on a short lease, built a summer house in which to entertain his friends while watching passing ships on the river, and planted poplars for shade.

Scenes from the film *Blow Up* were filmed in the park in the 1960s, and the park hasn't changed much since then. Birch, hornbeam, ash and oak trees and hawthorn now cover most of the Mount and the sides of the former quarries, while the summit of the Mount is grassland. The acid grassland on top of the ridge supports bright yellow gorse and other appropriate plants which also encourage insects in this lonely area.

The Greenwich Council plant nursery once stood close to the Lodge on Maryon Road and is now an organic food–growing garden with a community orchard, Forest School and teaching area, and part of the Capital Growth network

Maryon Wilson Park

The beautiful Maryon Wilson Park lies against the side of the escarpment in two wooded valleys with a central ridge and two little streams. Woodland walks pass sessile and pedunculate oaks, silver birches, ash trees, a Caucasian wingnut and hawthorns, and grassy glades with wildflowers. The park is particularly lovely in the autumn, when the leaves on the trees glow in the soft light, and even a short walk takes away worries and cares

Sheep and goats, two pigs, and ducks live in the animal enclosure, in the company of fallow deer. And three hard–working ponies give rides to people with disabilities at the riding facility next to Charlton Park Academy.

Access: Maryon Road SE7 8DH, Thorntree Road SE7 8AE
Opening times: Maryon Park — check website;
Maryon Wilson Park is always open
Facilities: Benches, children's playground, tennis courts, basketball court, Community Garden
Designation: Maryon Park is a Green Flag Public Park; both parks are SINCs of Borough Importance Grade I
Size: 25 hectares (62 acres)
Friends of Maryon Parks: www.friendsofmaryonparks.org

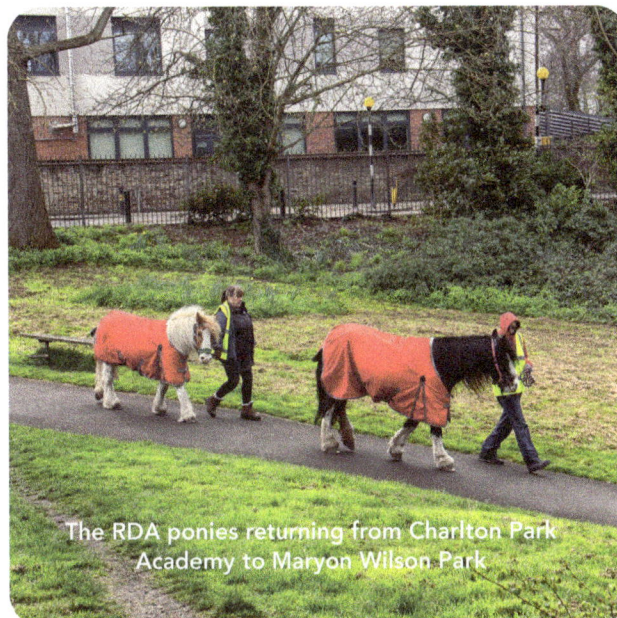
The RDA ponies returning from Charlton Park Academy to Maryon Wilson Park

36

Hello! Animal Farm in Maryon Wilson Park

Maryon Wilson Park in late November
(both pages)

St Luke's Church

A flagstone path leads from the entrance gate on the main road to the church. The small churchyard, now closed to burials, has gravestones set among grass, and yew and hornbeam trees shield the building from the roads. If you visit, be sure to walk round the east end of the church to the quiet garden behind the building, away from the traffic, and just sit and reflect in the calmness.

The original St Luke's Church was built of chalk and flint in the 12th century. It stood at the top of Charlton Church Lane which leads down to Anchor and Hope Lane, an ancient Manway across the marshes to the Thames. The Abbey of Bermondsey controlled the church until the Dissolution of the Monasteries in the 16th century.

St Luke's was largely rebuilt in 1630–39 with a bequest from Sir Adam Newton of Charlton House. There was further work in the 19th and 20th centuries and today it is Grade II* listed.

In the past, the church's tower was a navigation aid for naval cadets training on the river, and so the church is allowed to fly the pre–1800 ensign on St George's and St Luke's days.

The Charlton War Memorial is nearby, at the junction of Charlton Church Lane and Charlton Park Road where there is a cattle trough and drinking fountain. Both were built to commemorate the King's coronation in 1902.

Amongst the many important memorials in the church are those of Sir Adam Newton and Spencer Perceval, the only British Prime Minister to be assassinated. Burials in the crypt include members of the Maryon–Wilson and Langhorne families.

Access: Charlton Church Lane SE7 8UG
Opening times: Churchyard always open
Facilities: Bench
Designation: Churchyard
Size: 0.2 hectares (0.5 acres)
Charlton Church: https://charlton.church

37

116

St Thomas Churchyard

A group of dedicated volunteers have worked hard to transform the small churchyard into an oasis of delight around the church.

A beautiful pink rose greets you at the gate, and the path guides you past daisies, buttercups and small pink wildflowers flourishing in the grass to the west door of the church. An abundant garden is establishing itself here around an interesting bench built from the wood of HMS Arethusa. Gravestones have been uncovered from a previous mass of brambles, and broken tombstones have been formed into a wall at one end of the garden.

There are several interesting tombs: Walter de la Mare was born in Maryon Road, and although he is buried in St Paul's, the family tomb is here. At the east end, the gravestones stand in a wildflower meadow where a solitary Kipling stone remembers a sailor on HMS Cumberland, which was a convoy escort ship in WWI.

Joseph Gwilt designed the church, and Sir Thomas Maryon–Wilson, 6th Baronet, the main funder, laid the foundation stone in 1849. The church was consecrated in 1850 and closed for burials in 1933.

Access: Woodland Terrace SE7 8EW
Opening times: Garden always open
Facilities: Benches
Designation: Churchyard
Size: 0.3 hectares (0.7 acres)
St Thomas Church: https://southwark.anglican.org/church/old-charlton-st-thomas/

Opposite: *The bench made from the wood of HMS Arethusa*

38

WOOLWICH

Woolwich "is a place for sight-seekers to glory in," says Bradshaw in 1862,[31] and even Baedeker added Woolwich to his list of London sights in 1881. Today, Woolwich remains an intriguing, chameleon–like area and the administrative centre for the Royal Borough of Greenwich

Nearly 2,500 years ago, Woolwich, or Hulviz, Wollewic, Wulewiche, or Wlewic amongst other spellings, was a Celtic settlement on the River Thames near today's Free Ferry, and because it was fortified, it was probably an important settlement. The people fished and the name (wic) suggests a trading port, perhaps trading in wool. North Woolwich was on the opposite side of the river until 1965 (and is now part of the Borough of Newham), so could there have been a ferry across the river to link the sheep–farming tradition in East Anglia with the Celtic settlement to facilitate trade?

Later, Roman artefacts and burial sites were found here and a track — Sandy Hill Road? Cholic Lane? — connected the settlement with the Roman Road over Shooters Hill.

The Saxons followed the Romans and built a small church on the hill above the river. The villagers fished for "troutes and sauman, pikes, roches, barbils, and other fish,"[32] beaching their flat–bottomed boats on the shore and trading from them, and they made their own pottery. Life rolled on even when ownership of the land changed.

King Alfred's daughter gifted Woolwich to the Abbey of St Peter in Ghent in 918. She had married Baldwin II, Count of Flanders, and both are buried in that Abbey. The estate changed hands several times between the Crown and the Abbey until the repossession of all the Alien Priories in 1414, when Henry V gave the estates to the Priory of Sheen in Richmond. At the Dissolution of the Monasteries in the 16th century, all land reverted to the Crown.

Then, in 1514, Henry VIII established a Royal Dockyard to build warships including his flagship *Henry Grace à Dieu*. (The previous year he had founded the dockyard in Deptford.) A gun store and a ropeyard followed (today's Beresford Street). A Board of Ordnance controlled the establishment as a modern–day 'Ministry of Defence'.

From this point, Woolwich grew in importance as an industrialised garrison town and the largest producer of armaments in England in its time. A less publicised fact was the use of convict labour for the hardest work in the factories, the unfortunate souls being housed in two ships moored in the river.

As always, there were powerful men associated with development. Sir Robert Mansell (1573–1656) managed the dockyard and the ropeyard but also owned two glass factories at Glass Yard, which had a monopoly on glass manufacture in the country. Kilns produced Bellarmine stoneware and earthenware and clay pipes, and sand was quarried in the nearby sandpits.

In the 1530s, Sir Martin Bowes, a wealthy goldsmith and important figure in the Royal Mint, started buying land in Woolwich and Plumstead. He built his home, Tower Place,

Entrance to the former dockyards

One of the two former dry docks

close to the Thames. The land to the east was a rabbit warren where the Board of Ordnance tested guns, and in 1671 the Board bought the land.

In 1696, the Laboratory was set up to make ammunition; the Royal Brass Foundry started making guns in 1717; the Royal Carriages Department built gun carriages; and there was a storekeepers depot. The Artillery Regiment was formed here in 1716, with barracks onsite and the Royal Academy followed in 1741 in Tower Place. Manufacturing expanded rapidly, driven by demands of war, and the barracks and the academy were forced to move to new buildings on Woolwich Common in the 19th century.

Despite the importance of the dockyard, there were disadvantages to its situation: the river silted up, the geology of the site was difficult, and there were ongoing problems with the workforce. In 1969, the dockyard closed. Most of the area was redeveloped as a housing estate in the following years, leaving only the Superintendent's house and office (1778-84), the 19th century gates in the walls and two dry docks of 1843 (filled in) as reminders of the past. It is a bleak area today with no green spaces for the residents and no trees to soften the landscape.

The town benefited from the military presence, but also struggled with poverty, and employment waxed and waned with Britain's wars. The Dusthole between the dockyard and the arsenal was one of the London's most notorious slums in the 19th century, with "low, narrow and dirty streets …. mean brick dwellings and small shabby shops."[33]

The North Kent railway line opened in 1849, and in 1868, workers at the Arsenal established the Royal Arsenal Co–operative Society, one of the biggest in the country. In 1889, Woolwich became part of London rather than Kent, and in 1965, it merged with the London Borough of Greenwich. Major changes only came post–WWII.

In 1967, the Arsenal closed down. The eastern part is today's Thamesmead, and in 1994 the MOD sold the western section to Berkeley Homes for redevelopment as Royal Arsenal Riverside (RAR).

Now, Woolwich is changing again, and the vision for the 21st century is of a residential, cultural and small business centre. Historical buildings have been renovated or converted to housing, so the past is not entirely forgotten; new and energy–efficient homes are being built, with varied green spaces; the old market is to be redeveloped; and there are good transport links to the centre of London.

These are some of the facts about Woolwich, but the rich tapestry of the individual lives which shaped the past cannot be explored in this small space, and so I recommend to you *The Woolwich Story* by E F E Jefferson.

Essential reading

www.royal-arsenal-history.com
Jefferson, E F E, *The Woolwich Story*, (1970, Instance Printers, (Woolwich) Ltd)
Saint, Andrew, *Survey of London, Vol.48, Woolwich*, (2012, Yale University Press)
Vincent, W T T, *Records of the Woolwich District, Vols 1 & II, 1890*, (2015, republished by FamLoc Books, Michael Wood (Editor))

Royal Arsenal Riverside (RAR)

39

Royal Arsenal Riverside (RAR) is a £1.2 billion regeneration project by Berkeley Homes over thirty years which started in 2001 and covers eighty–eight acres on the riverside. It is the largest site of Grade I and Grade II listed buildings converted to residential use in the UK and will provide 5,000 new homes when finally completed.

> "Housebuilding is about more than building houses. Regeneration schemes create new neighbourhoods, too, with distinct identities and a vibrant feel. Meanwhile, the whole site is now filling up nicely with shops, cafés, pubs and restaurants. There is [also] a regular farmers' market at Major Draper Street."

Citation for the Best Regeneration Project Award in the Evening Standard New Homes Awards in 2022.[34]

Today, this former industrial site incorporates new green spaces. The development along the Thames Path which stretches for 1 km along the river on the north of the site and the landscaping here has imaginative touches — intermittent fountains, little waterfalls, a remnant of old wall, colourful plants — this is a fun area in which to walk, and the lucky residents have additional private gardens.

Access: Woolwich SE18 6FR

Above: *Assembly of 2001 by Peter Burke*
Opposite: *Green spaces amongst the flats*

Dial Arch Square

The Verbruggen House

The Elizabeth Line Station in Woolwich opens on to a pretty green square surrounded by historical buildings, almost a village green. And just like a genuine village green, it has a pub, in fact two! It is a busy space, with a constant stream of life passing under the substantial London plane trees.

On the right is The Great Pile, which was built in 1717–20 as workshops. (This was once the site of a Roman cemetery.) The engineers who worked here formed the Dial Square Football Club in 1886; two years later this became the Royal Arsenal Football Club, and in 1891, when the club turned professional, it became the Woolwich Arsenal Football Club. The final change came in 1913 when the Arsenal Football Club moved to Highbury.

The Dial Arch Pub

The Royal Brass Foundry

Today, only the frontage of The Great Pile remains. In 1764, this carried a sundial, which is probably the origin of the square's name, and the building is now the Dial Arch pub.

To your left is the Verbruggen House. Jan Verbruggen and his son Pieter came to Woolwich in 1770 to run the Royal Brass Foundry. Jan Verbruggen was born in West Friesland and worked for the Admiralty and the Foundry in the Hague where he developed new techniques for making cannons. He brought this knowledge to England, and later it was essential to the development of steam engines. Father and son were appalled by the existing accommodation and built themselves a new house which today is offices.

And straight ahead is the Main Guardhouse of 1788, a Grade II listed building by James Wyatt. Now it is a pub of the same name and it stands alongside the Royal Brass Foundry.

The Royal Brass Foundry of 1716–17 was the first building designed to manufacture guns for both the army and the navy. The Master Founder was Andrew Schalch who came from Switzerland to establish the Foundry. He was replaced by the Verbruggens who extended the building. It is is a rare example of a purpose–built foundry and workshop.

Access: Woolwich SE18 6GH
Opening Times: Always open
Facilities: Benches
Designation: Public Open Space

The Future Maribor Park

The Temporary Park was a substantial and attractive open green park, with a wildflower meadow and young trees on undulating ground criss–crossed with paths. Sadly, however, the park has been dug up and will be replaced with tower blocks of flats.

Instead, Maribor Park will be a four–acre linear park aligned with Beresford Street and incorporating a water feature which links the town centre to the river.

"The vision for the park focuses on creating spaces which celebrate … historic themes such as warrens, kilns and ropemaking" while creating "a rich biodiverse landscape."[35] Beresford Street was once the ropeyard.

A tiny paved space hidden alongside the Foundry is 'The Source', the start of the linear water park. It is very attractive, but it causes problems because the sides of the water feature are not graded and so the little ducklings who visit cannot escape, and have to be rescued.

From 'The Source' the water will run into the new Maribor Park and down to 'The Delta.' Children love playing in the water here on a hot summer's day, but where will they run round and kick a ball now that the open space of the Temporary Park has gone?

Access: Woolwich SE18 6BG
Facilities: Benches at 'The Source', seating at 'The Delta'

Left above: *The Delta*
Below: *The Source*
Opposite: *The former Temporary Park and the building site*

Wellington Park

Wellington park is an elegant formal park which is cleverly built over an underground car park — please can we see more of these garden car parks?

The park is named after the Duke of Wellington who was Master General of the Ordnance from 1818–27 and his statue originally stood at the Tower of London where the Board of Ordnance was based. The Board was responsible for supplying arms and ammunition to the army and navy. The statue was moved to the Arsenal in 1863 and to the park in 2005. The statue of 1848 is by Thomas Milnes and it is Grade II listed.

The park is bordered by historical buildings.

The Shot and Shell Foundry of 1856 once stood here, and its imposing entrance gatehouse is still in place. It is a Grade II listed building which has been converted into flats. And the Grand Store of 1806–13 to the north, which provided extraordinarily grand, even palatial, storage for army equipment, has also been carefully renovated for housing.

Wellington Park is a welcome expanse of green grass and open space amongst imposing and massive buildings.

Access: Hastings Street SE18 6TE
Opening times: Always open
Facilities: Benches
Designation: Public Park
Size: 1 hectare (2.5 acres)

39c

Above: *The Duke of Wellington in front of the Gatehouse to the Shot and Shell Foundry*
Opposite: *The park above the car park in winter, with the Grand Store in the background*

Royal Military Barracks

By the mid–1700s, the army had outgrown its training facilities and accommodation in The Warren on the Thames. So, in 1773, the Board of Ordnance bought the northern part of the Common and enclosed the land behind Ha–Ha Road to build the Royal Artillery Barracks.

The Royal Regiment of Artillery was headquartered in the barracks until 2007, and the military are scheduled to leave finally in 2028, but the future of the buildings is unclear. They are Grade II* listed.

Barrack Field

Barrack Field is just south of the parade ground and the barracks. A ha–ha or boundary ditch separates the field from Woolwich Common and was built to stop animals straying into military grounds. In the 18th century, it was home to Woolwich Cricket Club. Today, the field is divided by a fence and the footpath dividing the field is often closed to the public.

Below: *The Royal Military Barracks SE18 4BH, and the side of St George's Garrison Church in winter*

Repository Woods

"The Royal Military Repository at Woolwich was developed by Lt General Sir William Congreve (1743–1814) as a school of methods of mounting and dismounting ordnance."[36] As a Captain in the Royal Artillery, he had fought in Canada in the Seven Years War (1756–63) and found soldiers struggled to move and position guns in unfamiliar terrain.

So, in Woolwich, he developed a programme of manoeuvring guns over ditches and crossing rivers using mechanical means. These training grounds were probably available by 1775. The landscape in Repository Woods was naturally hilly and included a small stream; the large pond dates from 1808; and there were two smaller ponds as well, with a network of paths and tracks, ditches, batteries and earthworks.

The Rotunda, a Grade II* listed building, was built by John Nash as a ballroom in the grounds of Carlton House in 1814. The occasion was the meeting of the allied sovereigns to celebrate the defeat and abdication of Napoleon Bonaparte. The Prince Regent asked for it to be moved to Woolwich and this was completed in 1820.

It was clearly a very attractive site, and important visitors and the general public were welcomed at opening times as a PR exercise by the military, and to show off the professionalism of the army.

The site was a training ground until the late 1850s, after which time it was too small for the increasingly large weapons. Today, the area is woodland and closed to the general public, although The Dell Angling Society is fortunate to have restricted access to the large pond.

The woods, of 2.8 hectares (7 acres), lie behind the Royal Military Barracks and alongside Hillreach Road SE18 4AL, and are a SINC of Borough Importance Grade I.

41

The Dell Angling Society enjoying a day's fishing in Repository Woods

Academy Place Reservoirs & Playing Fields

The original Academy was in The Warren where it replaced Martin Bowes' Tower Place in 1718–23. The building still overlooks Artillery Place, which is the site of a busy weekend market. But when the Barracks moved up to the Common in 1803, the Academy followed in 1806.

By the 1990s, the Academy was no longer suitable for the army, and the site, excluding the former married quarters on both sides of Prince Imperial Road, was sold to Durkan Estates in 2006 for redevelopment as private housing.

The land between the Academy and Shooters Hill, known as Jacob's Corner, was leased in the 1840s–50s to the Labourers' Friend Society and used for gardens or allotments. Lord Shaftesbury founded the Society in 1830 to improve living conditions for working people on low incomes. The Society was one of the Model Dwellings Companies and built houses, but also encouraged the use of allotments. The Society was finally taken over by the Peabody Trust.

The Kent Water Works Company bought the Ravensbourne Waterworks in Lewisham in 1805–09. The company supplied Deptford, Lee, Greenwich, Lewisham and Rotherhithe with water from the Ravensbourne, and also supplied Woolwich.

In 1844, the company dug a circular reservoir on the west side of Academy Road to supply Woolwich Dockyard, particularly in case of fire.

In 1872, they dug another, square reservoir on the east side of the road which was covered and is fenced off. The reservoir is still visible today.

In 1911–12, the War Office gave the Academy the waterlogged grounds south of today's Prince Imperial Road. The land was drained and football, rugby and hockey pitches and a running track were created for the sole use of students at the Academy.

The reservoir and playing field are a surprise, bounded by two very busy main roads, yet they remain peaceful. Walk along the path below the playing fields, near the entrance from the A205, and you will be astonished by what you find.

Access: Prince Imperial Road SE18 4JE and Academy Place SE18 4AA
Opening times: Always open
Facilities: None
Designation: Amenity Green Space
Size: 1.75 hectares (2.5 acres

42

The Academy's Church of St Michael and All Angels

A cricket match on the grounds in front of the former Academy

The covered reservoir (above), remains of firing butts (below), and the fields in late autumn (opposite)

Woolwich Common

Woolwich Common had been Common Land owned by the Crown since time immemorial. Local people grazed their cattle here and the land supplied them with fuel — turf, wood, and gorse. It used to be much bigger, stretching from Charlton Cemetery to Shooters Hill. But as the Royal Arsenal expanded on its riverside site to meet demands of Empire and war, the open land came under threat.

The Board of Ordnance already used the Common for testing guns in the early 1700s and later for artillery practice. By 1801, there was an increasing fear of invasion during the Napoleonic Wars and an Act of Parliament gave the Board full control of Woolwich Common and Charlton Common as part of a plan to fortify London. Finally, in 1803, the Board bought Charlton Common (102 acres) from the Maryon–Wilson family and then Woolwich Common from the Crown, and much of the ground was levelled.

However, times were changing. The Commons Preservation Society was founded in 1865; the Metropolitan Commons Act was passed in 1866; and the Plumstead riots secured Plumstead Common as open land for posterity. In this context, a campaign by Rev J W Horsley forced the military to allow more public access to open land.

By the 1860s, the northern part of the area was already regarded as a 'People's Park' where the locals walked and played games in the summer. In 1863, a drinking fountain was built in the north east corner, donated by Anna Victoria Little in memory of her husband, Major Robert John Little.

The Common is divided into two by a low embankment.

The southern half of the site is raised; blitz rubble covered with imported soil has encouraged neutral grassland and scrub. It is surrounded by secondary woodland with mature black and white poplar trees on the western side and more mixed woodland in the south and in the east, planted after WWII.

A small wetland in the south east corner was the site of a reservoir belonging to the Kent Water Works company and is covered with reeds, and alders and willows stand nearby.

The northern part is quite different, being hard, level ground, the sands and gravels which were the original surface of the Common. This is acid grassland which is now rare in London.

There are clumps of wild flowers around the Common which is the only known site for wild tare in London.

Yes, Woolwich Common is surrounded by busy main roads, but you can forget the traffic as you walk along the tree–lined perimeter path, particularly in the south, or thread your way through a dense copse in the centre of the Common. In the late summer there is an abundance of blackberries, and there are even two apple trees! This is a wonderful open space in which to walk in the open air, and for our pleasure we owe thanks and gratitude to the Friends, who pick up litter and keep a watchful eye.

Access: A205 road SE18 4DE, Stadium Road, Ha–Ha Road
Opening times: Always open
Facilities: The Capital Ring Path and Green Chain Walk cross the Common
Designation: Metropolitan Open Land, SINC of Borough Importance Grade I
Size: 45 hectares (111 acres)
Friends of Woolwich Common: https://friendsofwoolwichcommon.org.uk

43

Woolwich Common in July looking towards the Academy and Shooters Hill

Perennial sweetpea and wild carrot seed head

St Mary Magdalene Church Gardens

The church gardens are a welcome and attractive green space in the centre of Woolwich, although somewhat separated from the town by main roads.

Shortly after the Conquest, the small church in the Saxon fishing village was replaced with a stone building dedicated to St Lawrence. In 1100, King Henry I gave the church to the Priory and Convent of St Andrew in Rochester. Henry V passed the church to the Carthusian Priory of Sheen in Richmond in 1414. By the 15th century, the church was dedicated to the Virgin Mary, and a century later it was dedicated to St Mary Magdalene.

But by the 17th century, the building was in danger because a new road to service the expanding dockyard ate into the sloping ground next to the church, destabilising the building and destroying the graveyard. Local residents warned the Admiralty that "the bones of the dead are washed out of the churchyard and into the river."[37]

A century later, with the help of fundraising and a small donation from the Fifty New Churches Act of 1711, the old church and ossuary were demolished and rebuilt higher up the hill on land bought from the Bowater family, the main landowners in this area. The churchyard was enlarged in later years but finally closed for burials in 1855.

The church was used as a semaphore station at the end of the 1700s and as late as 1847.

Charles Escreet was appointed Vicar in 1892. Isabella Holmes identified him as "a new race of clergy...[who] no sooner came into possession of their livings than they wrote to the Association, begging that their churchyards might be taken in hand."[38]

The Metropolitan Public Gardens Association converted the four–acre graveyard into a public garden laid out by Fanny Rollo Wilkinson. She was the first professional woman landscape designer and also worked with Octavia Hill's Kyrle Society. J Passmore Edwards underwrote the work, and the local Board of Health took on the upkeep.

The gravestones were stacked against the perimeter walls, new gravel paths were laid down and trees and shrubs created an English parkland. A drinking fountain was installed and a viewing platform to the north of the church looked out over the river. HRH the Duchess of Fife opened the new Woolwich Gardens in 1895. Sadly, the view over the river is now compromised by high–rise flats.

In the early 1960s, the gardens were enlarged and redesigned by GP Youngman, the council's Consultant Landscape Architect. He added raised beds, alpine rockeries and new paths, and more gravestones were moved to the perimeter.

Only the tomb of Tom Cribb (1781–1848) remains in situ. George Borrow wrote worshipfully of the world champion bare–knuckle fighter as "perhaps the best man in England … with his huge massive figure, and face wonderfully like that of a lion."[39] And that is what his tomb depicts!

Be warned! The church has a resident flock of pigeons which will pursue you relentlessly until you deliver suitable nourishment!

Access: Greenlaw Street SE18 5NB and
John Wilson Street SE18 6JP
Opening times: Gardens always open
Facilities: Benches
Designation: Grade II* listed building and public garden, SINC of Local Importance
Size: 1.9 hectares (4 acres)
St Mary's Church: www.stmaryswoolwich.co.uk

44

The rear of the church with a glimpse of the children's playground, Tom Cribb's tomb, and the pesky pigeons!

THAMESMEAD

Thamesmead is the most extraordinary and surprising area in the Royal Borough of Greenwich, in my view. Not only does the green infrastructure document, *Living in the Landscape*, quote Roger Deakin, but the management is guided by a humane vision of the interaction between people and their surroundings, based on the legacy of one man, George Peabody.

"Thamesmead is not only the biggest regeneration project in London but one of the biggest in the UK. Peabody know that the quality of a place is hugely important, and that happiness and health is intimately related to the places where people live and work, and a poor–quality environment has a huge impact on people's lives. They recognise the value of using nature–based solutions to create." Or in the words of John Lewis, Executive Director of Thamesmead, "What is special about Thamesmead .. is the spaces between buildings."[40]

George Peabody (1795–1869) came from a poor family in America and had little formal education. He was apprenticed at eleven years old and made himself into a businessman and financier. In 1837 he moved to London, but he never forgot his roots and the deprivations of his childhood.

Peabody made donations of over $8 million in his lifetime, not by handing out cash to people, but by establishing and endowing permanent foundations in the USA which support education and scientific research, and museums, libraries and historical societies. And he expected the institutions to be run to the highest professional standards.

In London, he founded the Peabody Donation Fund in 1862 to provide good quality rented housing for working people of sound character who were on modest incomes. The housing encouraged a sense of community and included play areas for children. The first Peabody building opened on Commercial Street, Spitalfields, in 1864 but has been sold. Peabody's oldest estate is the Islington Estate of 1865 on Greenman Street.

The original charity has absorbed other organisations over the years, and expanded, but today the Peabody Trust still continues his original aims. Yes, they believe in collaboration and consult with the residents of the estates, but the management shares Peabody's vision of people as dignified human beings, mindful of themselves and others and considerate towards their surroundings. They guide and encourage the residents towards that vision — the management leads behaviour and change.

George Peabody's statue behind the Royal Exchange in the City

Thamesmead is built on former marshes with an interesting history.

In 1279, the monks of Lesnes Abbey enclosed the marshes and so became responsible for maintaining the seawall. However, there were two major breaches in 1527 in Plumstead and Erith. In the 1560s, Jacob Acontius undertook to drain the marshes in return for land for himself, but it was many years before all the land was recovered and even then it was vulnerable to flooding at very high tides.

The Royal Woolwich Arsenal was established in Woolwich in the 16th century and spread eastwards into The Warren where the open land used for weapons testing and storage of ammunition. (See section on Woolwich.) Further east, the Plumstead marshes were farmed or left untouched. The military presence continued into the 20th century until finally, in the 1960s, the ammunition dumps were cleared.

At this point, the GLC selected the area for redevelopment as a 'town for the 21st century' providing public and private housing, amenities and work for 60,000 people. The vision was grand, with modern architecture and sympathetic landscaping which included canals and water features. The first three phases were completed by 1975 but were not completely successful.

In 2000, a new governance structure was put in place, with Gallions Housing Association, Trust Thamesmead and Tilfen Land in joint control. In 2014, all three organisations came together under Peabody, which today owns 65% of the land.

The seawall was raised in the 1960s and will be raised again by 2050. The marshy land is controlled through drainage ditches which have been transformed into canals, and the water is held in the lakes before flowing out into the Thames at low tides, or is pumped into the river if levels are unacceptably high. These measures enable the land to be used for housing in an imaginative way in line with the original vision for Thamesmead.

The environment is monitored through the Marsh Dykes and Thamesmead Catchment Action Plan.

"Thamesmead's landscape is remarkable. Its 240 hectares of parks and green space, seven kms of canals, five lakes, five kms of river frontage and 53,000 trees, sets it apart from any other urban area in the UK. Here, residents enjoy more than double the amount of green space than the average Londoner."[41] There are fourteen Sites of Interest for Nature Conservation, (SINCs), with various habitats and plants species, which support numerous birds, insects and animals.

The residents are very fortunate to live in such richly natural surroundings close to the centre of London. I suggest the way to explore Thamesmead is to start at one of the lakes and then explore the canals around the lake in linear or circular walks.

Essential reading:

Living in the Landscape, 2021, www.peabody.org.uk
Parker, Franklin, *George Peabody: A Biography*, (1971, Vanderbilt University Press)

Birchmere Lake & Park

Birchmere Lake is an excellent fishing lake set in parkland and is also a beautiful place to walk.

The lake was made in the 1970s and is 5–7 feet deep. It was restocked with c.250 carp in 2015 as well as tench, bream, rudd and roach, and the biggest carp weigh over 15 lbs! It is popular with anglers and fishing is organised by the Thamesmead Town Angling Club.

There is secondary woodland on the southern side of the lake, forming a barrier to the busy Eastern Way, and the lake edge is planted with large reedbeds which include great reedmace, galingale and common club rush. Lesser water–parsnip and round–fruited rush, both rare in London, can also be found.

Swans, mallards, moorhens and terns are common, and reed warblers and blue kingfishers nest here. Dragonflies are plentiful.

Birchmere Park is next to the lake and is one of the first parks in Thamesmead where Peabody has planted hundreds of new trees. It stretches out along the Eastern Way from the lakeside and includes a maze, hidden green spaces, ball courts and a children's playground, ending with a community centre, orchard and garden. The main park is a sports field which also hosts a popular Sunday boot sale.

Access: Chervil Mews SE28 8EQ and Epstein Road SE28 8EJ
Opening times: Always open
Facilities: Green Chain Walk in the east of the lake, playing fields, fishing stands, benches, cricket and football pitches, basketball court, weekly Sunday boot sale, Community Hub and Garden
Designation: SINC Borough Importance Grade I
Size: 20 hectares (49 acres) park and lake

45

Birchmere Lake

Family fishing in Birchmere Lake

A Circular Walk of c.3 kms (1.9 miles)

From the eastern corner of Birchmere Lake, the Birchmere Drain East, one of the original drains on the marshes, leads to the Tump 53 Nature Reserve, and from there Butts Canal passes Butts Wood and Hawksmoor Park to reach Thamesmere Lake and the riverside shopping centre. Here there are several cafés. On the opposite side of the shopping centre is West Lake and the Twin Tumps from where the Waterfield Canal or West Drain leads back into the northern corner of Birchmere Lake. The combination of waterways, parks and lakes is a very enjoyable and easy circular walk.

Birchmere Drain East (L),
children in Tump 53 Nature Reserve
and
swans in Butts Canal

Tump 53 Nature Reserve

The tumps were ammunition storage facilities in the former Woolwich Arsenal, and they were numbered so that the railways could easily service them. By the early 1950s, there were still 40,000 tonnes of explosives stored in the Arsenal, enough to flatten a vast area of East London, and it was only in 1962 that the area was cleared.

Tump 53 was Magazine no.14 in which the Army Ordnance Corps stored cordite. Today it is in a small nature reserve, and a SINC of Borough Importance Grade I, (like the Twin Tumps) which is used for educational purposes and is a mix of grass and woodlands, surrounded by a moat. Over sixty varieties of birds have been found here, including kingfishers, willow warblers and redpolls.

Butts Wood

Butts Wood is named after the remains of the firing butts in this area. There is a large small–arms firing range wall next to the Woolwich Polytechnic School for Boys, and a curved wall behind the maze. Butts Wood maze was once Tump 54 or Magazine no.15, which was used for bulk storage of cordite. Lots of blackberries in Butts Wood in high summer!

Hawksmoor Park

Hawksmoor Park, of 2.5 hectares (6 acres), is alongside Butts Wood and there is no obvious reason for the name.

Thamesmere Lake

Thamesmere Leisure Centre overlooks the lake.

West Lake

Walk across the shopping centre to find the lake alongside the river. To the west are the Twin Tumps or Magazines nos.16 and 17 for the storage of bulk cordite and cartridges.

Twin Tumps Canal or West Drain

The West Drain, another drainage ditch, leads back through housing to the northern corner of Birchmere Lake.

46d
46e
46f

Remains of firing butts in Butts Wood

149

Hill (Tump?) in Hawksmoor Park

Butts Canal near the shopping centre

Butts Canal at the shopping centre with the base of the Clock Tower

West Lake

Crossway Park

Crossway Park is one of three large parks in Thamesmead.

The drainage ditch of the Crossway Canal was dammed to create a small, pretty lake in a delightfully varied park. The ground is undulating in parts, with groves of trees, a community orchard, a willow bed, children's playground and sports facilities. The Green Chain Walk crosses the park.

Access: Glendale Way SE28 8HA
Opening times: Always open
Facilities: Benches, tennis courts, playground, sports pitches, community orchard
Designation: Public Park, Lake is a SINC
Size: 14.3 hectares (35 acres)

A Circular Walk c.2 kms (1.2 miles)

The Crossway Canal leads from the lake in Crossway Park to **Moat Gardens** which was once Tump 52 or Magazine no.13 for bulk cordite in the Arsenal. The Gardens are always open and in the centre, surrounded by trees, is an attractive little skate park which is apparently a very good ride!

Follow the canal round to the left to find the small park of **Manorway Green** on Tump 47, the former Magazine no.9 for bulk cordite. It is now a pretty, green, wooded space with a children's playground. Continue down the canal back to the main road and then cross to Poplar Place or Glendale Way to find **Crossway Park.**

Or you can follow the path from **Manorway Green** a short distance to **the Thames.**

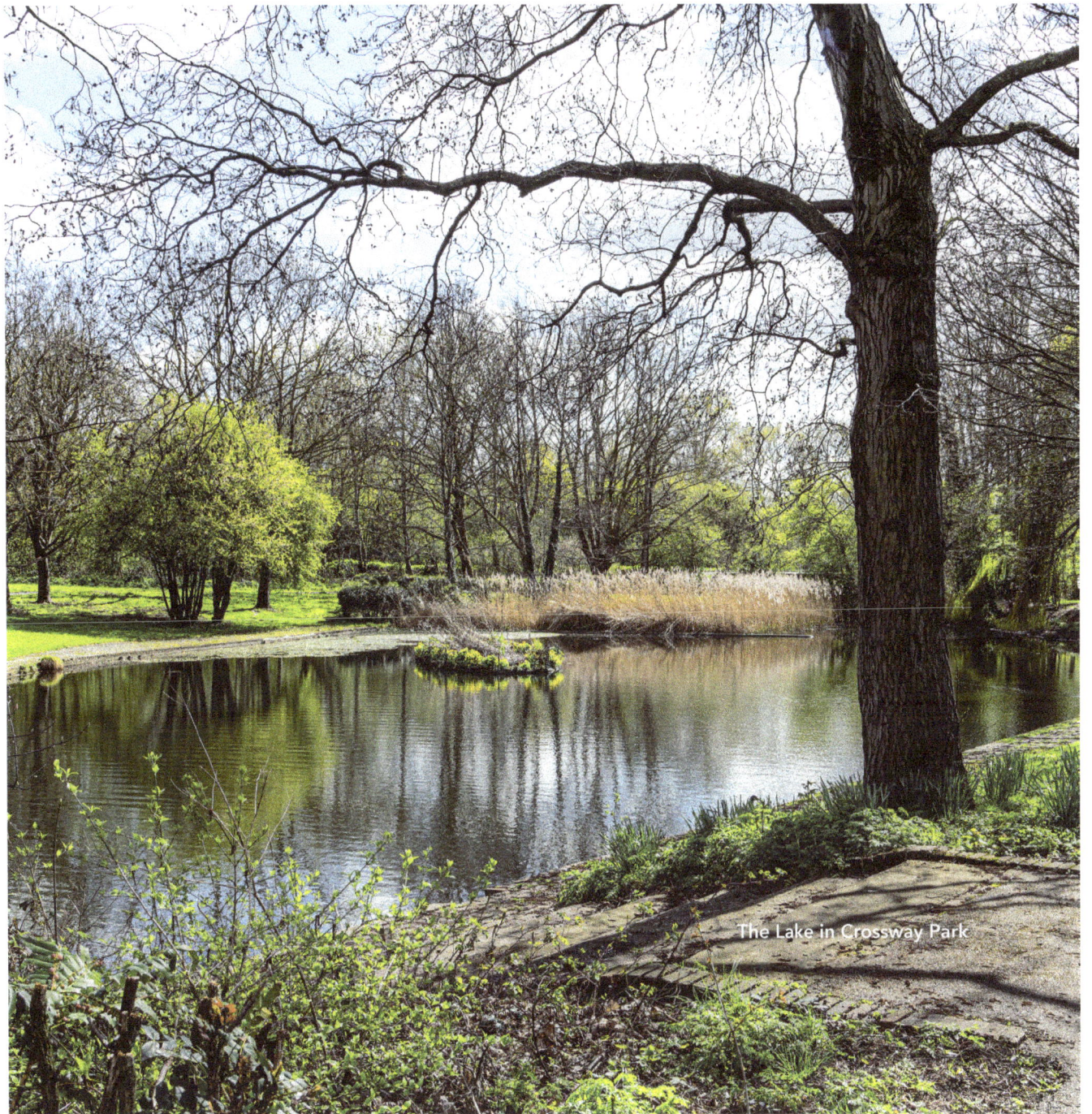

The Lake in Crossway Park

The skate park in Moat Gardens

The Crossway Canal

Canal junction at Moat Gardens

Children's playground in Manorway Park

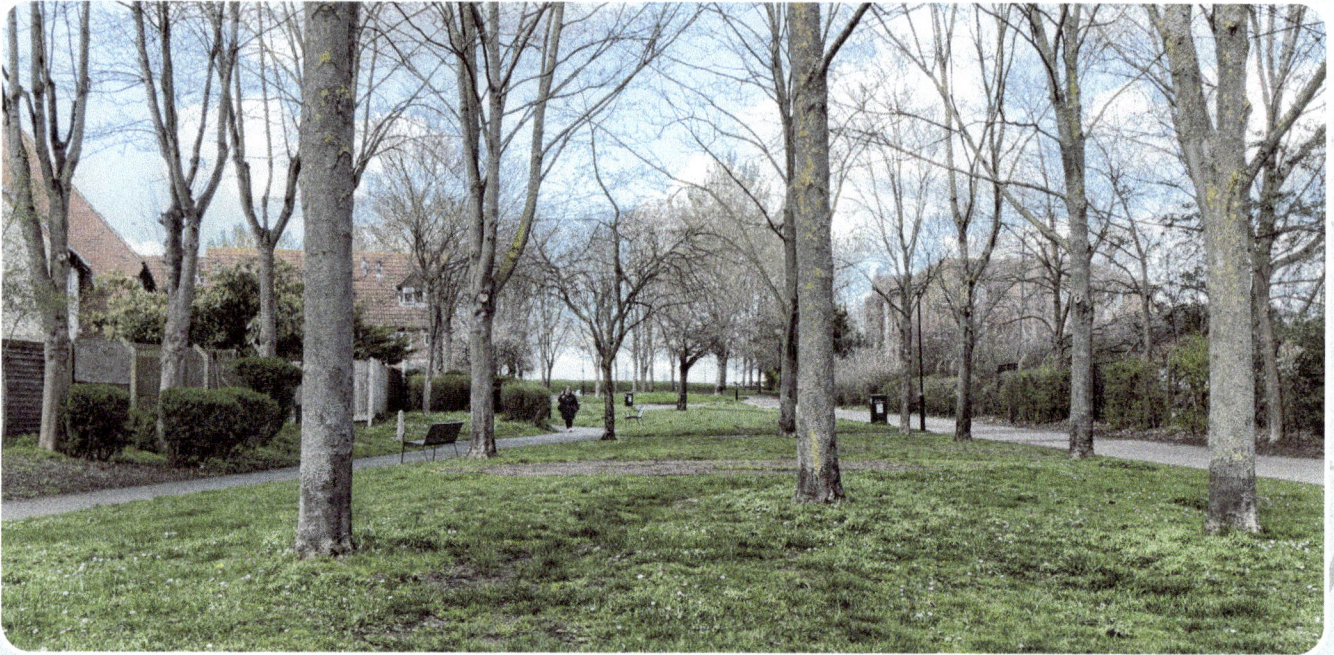

Above: The path to the Thames from Manorway Green, and **Below:** The Thames looking towards London

Thamesmead Ecology Study Area

Start at the lake in **Crossway Park**, follow the **Crossway Canal to Moat Gardens** where the canal divides. Turn right along the waterway to find the **Thamesmead Ecology Study Area,** which is not open to the general public. This was once Tump 39, Magazine no.5 for cordite and cartridges.

Today, the area supports a heronry and great crested grebes have been seen here, as well as mallards and coots. Wind your way through the housing to find the mouth of the canal at the Thames. This is a linear walk of c.1.5 kms and you will need a map.

Left: Canons at the mouth of the canal on the Thames
Below: Canal around the Study Area

49

Crossway Boardwalk & Wetlands

Crossness Boardwalk and Wetlands is a rectangular area of grasslands and water which stretches from the eastern side of Crossway Park to the Thames, and it will be retained in this natural state. On the west is housing, and in the east the Ridgeway is on the boundary with the Crossness Pumping Station. This was the Thamesmead Golf Course which closed in 2014.

The Ridgeway is a 5.6 kms (3.5 miles) linear walk, six metres above road level, from Plumstead Station to Crossness Pumping Station on the Thames, and the track is a mix of gravel and grass which can be muddy in places. The walk runs along the top of the Southern Outfall Sewer which was built by Joseph Bazalgette after an outbreak of cholera in London in 1853 and 'The Great Stink' of 1858. The Greenway is a similar path in north London.

The Ridgeway Biodiversity Project 2023–28 aims to improve accessibility, appearance, enjoyment and biodiversity of the path. The emphasis will be on removing dense scrub and non–indigenous species, and restoring grassland, wild flora and fauna, and bare ground. Thames Water, which owns the sewer, and Cory Riverside Energy will fund the project.

Access to wetlands: Bayliss Avenue SE28 8NJ
Opening times: Always open
Facilities: None
Designation: Ridgeway SINC of Local Importance Grade II

The Ridgeway in
Crossway Boardwalk and Wetlands
in winter

Crossway Wetlands

The former clubhouse on the old golf course

Gallions Park

Apparently the park is named after the Galyon family which owned land here — in the 14th century!

The Royal Arsenal Canal (above) is across the road from the park. It was built in the early 19th century as a means of delivering goods into the Royal Arsenal. And the main traffic was from the Royal Gunpowder Mills at Waltham Abbey. The plan is to convert the canal into a new park, the Broadwater Dock Park.

51

Installing the filtration beds

Peabody commissioned LUC to design a children's play area which is unusual for its thoughtfulness, with different areas offering appropriate challenges to children of different ages. The playground uses the character of the woodland setting and feels natural rather than being a fenced off and bleak area of hard landscape, as with many children's playgrounds. And the impact assessment confirms the health and social benefits of the design.

The lake in the park is 3–5 feet in depth and offers coarse fishing on day tickets. It is stocked with various fish, including varieties of carp.

In February 2024, a new wetland system was created in Gallions Lake with the help of Thames21 and volunteers. Water from the roads and culverts runs into planted pools where the water flow is slowed down, allowing the sediment to sink.

The floating platforms are planted with plants chosen with the help of interested residents, and include sedges, loosestrife, ragged robin and marsh marigolds. There is additional appropriate and varied planting on the margins of the lake which provides habitation for the fish. The plants absorb and lock up nitrates and phosphates and release organic compounds. The decontaminated water then flows into the lake, canals and so to the Thames.

The system is working well, but the planting also looks absolutely gorgeous and has greatly enhanced the beauty of this park. Might this idea work at The Tarn?

Access: Whinchat Road SE28 0HW
Opening times: Always open
Facilities: Children's play area, seats, fishing lake
Designation: Public Park, SINC of Borough Importance Grade II
Size: 4.5 hectares (11 acres)

The filtration beds in August

A circular walk from Gallions Park via Gallions Reach Park, c.3 kms (1.9 miles)

From the north east corner of the lake, a little canal leads to Gallions Reach Park, (SINC of Borough Importance Grade II),which links with the Thames Path and from there back to the outlet of the Royal Arsenal Canal and Gallions Park.

Gallions Reach Park

This undulating and landscaped park of 3 hectares (7 acres) is on the Thames. The hills are not tumps, but manmade of rubble from a nearby housing estate. A spiral path winds up two of the hills giving views over the surrounds. There are small children's playgrounds near the houses, and groves of young trees near the Thames.

Tripcock Park

The area opposite Gallions Reach Park is currently fenced off and although it is earmarked for housing development, it will include a new park, Tripcock Park.

Just resting!

52a
52b

The canal/drain out of Gallions Lake towards the east

The 'tumps' in Gallions Reach Park in winter

Southmere Lake & Park

53

The ground here is historically marshland, but Southmere Lake was created in the late 1960s as part of the drainage system. It is a beautiful expanse of water fed from surface water, and the Marsh Dykes River which flows from it's sources on the higher ground of Lesnes Woods, Bostall Woods and Shooters Hill into the south west corner of the lake. From here, the water flows into the Thames through drainage ditches, now converted into picturesque canals. The Southmere Boat House is the clubhouse for the boating club on the lake.

Wetlands on the east side of the lake are designed to attract birds and wildlife, and floating reed beds carry colourful wildflowers such as loosestrife and flag irises, which provide cover for birds. Bat boxes have been installed and a sand martin nesting wall, as well as perches for kingfishers.

Many varieties of water birds live on the lake, including gulls, mallard, pochard, cormorant, common tern, shoveler, coot, mute swan, great crested grebe and tufted duck. And the fish in the lake include bream, carp, perch and eels.

The Tiny Forest was planted in February 2022 with indigenous trees such as alder, willow and hazel, but also more unusual trees like the wild service tree, goat willow and downy birch. It is the first such plantation in Thamesmead and part of 'Thamesmead Making Space for Nature' and 'CLEVER Cities' programmes.

Trees are planted close together — the Miyawaki Method — to encourage the rapid creation of an urban forest. Tree Keepers were appointed from the local community to monitor and measure the growth of the forest, similar to the guardians associated with Street Trees for Living, who commit to care for new trees for two years.

Southmere Park extends into the Erith marshes next to the lake and includes Woodland Way, where poplars are being replaced with indigenous trees. The woodlands follow the line of a drainage ditch and so the area is wet.

From Southmere Lake, a canal leads to Crossway Park from where two walks are described (see Crossway Park). Or you can walk to the Thames through the Crossway Wetlands.

Access: Hartstock Drive DA18 4DU
Opening times: Always open
Facilities: Boat house, benches
Designation: Southmere Lake SINC Grade II
Size: 17 hectares (42 acres)

Abbey Way to Lesnes Abbey SE2 9X

Abbey Way leads from the south east corner of the Southmere Lake to Lesnes Abbey. It is developing into a very attractive linear park, raised above the surrounding area of housing. The park is planted with spring bulbs, trees and grass, there are benches on which to sit, and playgrounds for children.

The Way of c.1.3 kms (0.8 milles) is very different to the linear park on the Greenwich Peninsula!

Richard de Luci was the Chief Justiciar under Henry II (roughly Prime Minister). He was complicit in the murder of Thomas à Becket and it is thought he founded the Augustinian Foundation of Lesnes Abbey in 1178 as a penance

The Abbey did not flourish. There were never more than twelve canons, the cost of maintaining the seawall was considerable, and it was poorly governed. In 1525, this was one of the first monasteries repossessed by Wolsey.

Henry VIII passed the Abbey into private ownership, and the last owner, Thomas Hawes, bequeathed the site to Christ's Hospital School in 1663. It was managed as a farm until 1930 when the LCC bought the site and opened the park. It is now managed by Bexley Borough Council.

54

Children's playground on Abbey Way

Above: *The old black mulberry tree at Lesnes Abbey in winter*
Below: *The nave in the ruins of Lesnes Abbey in early January*

PLUMSTEAD

In 1800, the small Kentish village of Plumstead clustered round the Church of St Nicholas and an early 18th century pub, the Plume of Feathers. The area was reasonably prosperous for its time, and the few buildings stood on the main road between Woolwich and Erith.

Fishing in the river yielded salmon, sturgeon, lampreys and whitebait, and there was grazing for sheep and cattle in the marshes, which, according to Hasted, covered c.1,000 acres in 1797. The marshes swarmed with birdlife, including partridges which could be shot for the pot.

Even a century later, James Thorne described "market gardens and the broad marshes by the Thames kept for grazing. There are chalk and sand pits, brick and tile works, and [commercial] kilns where drain-pipes, garden pots and sugar moulds are largely made."[42]

On the flat, raised ground above the marshes, the ninety acres of market gardens produced peas and corn, and c.100 acres of orchards were mainly planted with apples and cherries. In 1890 W T T Vincent talks of strawberry gardens and hedgerows filled with wild roses, and upland wooded areas which were coppiced. It must have been idyllic.

Over millions of years, the Thames laid down along its banks a dense clay, which was ideal for brickmaking. The clay was quarried in pits along the river; domestic ash and cinders were added to make the bricks harden more efficiently, while lime or chalk gave London bricks their distinctive yellow colour. Bricks were handmade by local makers such as William Dawson in Plumstead.

A thousand years ago, in 960, King Edgar gave the Manor of Plumstede to the Abbey of St Augustine in Canterbury. The name has various interpretations including 'the place where plums were grown' and W T T Vincent offers several more. The manor was briefly held by Odo, Bishop of Bayeux, after the Conquest but then returned to the Benedictine Abbey until the Dissolution of the Monasteries in the 16th century when all religious establishments were claimed by the Crown.

The big landowners in Plumstead before the 1800s were the Crown, Sir Edward Boughton, Sir Martin Bowes, Queen's College Oxford, the Clothworkers' Company and the Earls of Shrewsbury.

In 1539, Henry VIII gave Sir Edward Boughton the Manor of Plumstead. As clerk to Henry VIII, he also managed the estates of Lesnes Abbey. By 1736, John Michel of Richmond owned the manor, which he bequeathed with others of his possessions to Queen's College Oxford to support eight fellowships, four scholarships and four exhibitioners at the college. The gift included Plumstead Common.

Sir Martin Bowes was prominent in the Goldsmith's Company, Master of the Royal Mint and Mayor of London.

Plume of Feathers pub

Bramblebury House

the country's military needs. The country was at war throughout the 19th century in Europe (Napoleonic Wars, Peninsular War, Crimean War), Asia (Anglo–Chinese wars), and Africa (as part of the Scramble for Africa).

And secondly, in 1844, the London, Chatham and North Kent Railway Company started building a line from London to Woolwich. The Pattisons sold 'Pattison's Sandpit' for the Woolwich Arsenal Station which opened in 1849, and Plumstead Station followed in 1859.

New housing developed in stages.

The upmarket Burrage Estate dates from the 1850s–60s on Pattison family land; the British Land Company laid out the Herbert Estate c.1861 for a similar market. Prior to that, the area was the farm and West Plumstead Pottery of Charles Gates. The Barnfield Housing Estate is now on the site of the pottery. Workers at the Arsenal lived closer to the river. Finally, the Royal Arsenal Co–operative Society developed the Bostall estate between 1900 and 1914.

At the beginning of the 19th century, the population of Plumstead was c.1,000 people, but one hundred years later it was c.68,000.

Plumstead was in Kent until 1930 when it was incorporated into the London Borough of Woolwich (LBW) together with Woolwich and Eltham. In 1965, the LBW was incorporated into the London Borough of Greenwich.

A very wealthy man, he acquired lands in Kent including the Manor of Bostall and built Suffolk Place, so named because it was believed the Duke of Suffolk rented the house as a hunting lodge. Bostall Farm and Suffolk Place Farm were sold separately in the 1600s, but came together when the Royal Arsenal Co–operative Society bought the land in the late 1800s.

The Pattison family owned the Manor of Burwash, and by the 1800s this had become the Burrage Estate, a landscaped park which would be built over with housing.

The Clothworkers' Company acquired land in Woolwich and Plumstead in the 16th century and used the income to fund Christ's Hospital Charity School. The Old Vicarage, Bramblebury House, was built in 1790–93 on Clothworkers' Company land but, although it is a Grade II listed building, it has been converted into flats and the original interior is completely lost. The company's Plumstead properties were only finally sold in 1959 but the name lives on in Clothworkers' Wood near Shrewsbury Park.

The main driver of change in the 19th century was the expansion of the Woolwich Arsenal in response to

Essential reading:

Cowdell, Julia, *Our Common Story*, (2004, Plumstead Common Environment Group)
Vincent, W T T, *Records of the Woolwich District, Vol II*, (1890, republished by FamLoc, Michael Wood, (Editor))
Weightman, Colin, *Plumstead Stories*, (2006, www.plumstead–stories.com)

Bostall Gardens

Wow! Roger Federer was here!

The park was transformed in June 2023 when the tennis courts where refurbished and painted in a unique design by street artists Christoph and Florin Schmidt, the Low Bros from Berlin. And Roger Federer performed the opening ceremony!

Bostall Gardens has a long history as Bostall Farm in Kent, which probably dated back to the 16th or 17th century. Old photographs show Bostall Farmhouse was a typical weatherboarded Kent building.

In 1887, the Royal Arsenal Co–operative Society (RACS) bought the fifty–two–acre Bostall Farm for £6,200, and twelve years later added the adjacent 122 acres of Suffolk (Place) Farm in order to produce goods for sale in Co–op stores, and feed for horses and pigs. Cowsheds were converted to piggeries and tomatoes and cucumbers were grown in greenhouses.

But Plumstead was expanding eastwards, and the Royal Arsenal Co–operative Society (RACS) switched to property development, starting the construction of the Bostall housing estate in 1900. Luckily, the area of today's park was left as farmland. In 1938, the site was bought by the Woolwich Borough Council (whose arms remain on the gate) and after WWII, it was made into Bostall Gardens which opened in 1952. Terraced gardens were laid out with paths, flowers and lawns, and over time a bowling green and toilets were added. But in the 1980s, the bowling green closed and the park keeper left.

In the early 2000s, a group of local people worked with the council to restore the park. The bowls pavilion was converted to a community centre, and the bowling green was replaced with a children's playground and ball courts.

Today's Friends of Bostall Garden dates from 2019. The Friends work tirelessly for the local community: as well as litter picking, they are planting thousands of crocuses with schoolchildren, they host a community summer festival, and have installed bat and bird boxes. The council, and Friends, planted a mini community orchard in 2019 with apples, pears, plum, and cherry trees. Look out for a strawberry tree, a beautiful weeping ash tree and the magnificent hornbeam which is a glorious autumn sight in this cherished small park.

Access: Viola Avenue SE2 0TQ
Opening times: 9 am to dusk
Facilities: Community centre, benches, tennis courts, children's playground, outdoor gym gear
Designation: Public Park of 1 hectare (2.5 acres)
Friends of Bostall Gardens: www.facebook.com

55

Bostall Community Gardens

Bert

Visiting Bostall Community Garden is like going through the looking glass in Alice's Wonderland. It hides away behind a gate in one corner of Bostall Gardens, and it is lush, productive, and absolutely beautiful. This is undoubtedly one of the greenest green spaces in the Borough of Greenwich.

There is a small, 'proper' garden with trees, shrubs and flowers, and even in the autumn it is full of pretty things to see and enjoy. And it has a little corner where you can just sit quietly in the company of an elf, and Bert.

The fruit and vegetable area is a 'Wow!' The beds are immaculate and full of interesting vegetables. There are lines of fruit canes and fruit trees and a greenhouse for tender and exotic fruit and vegetables. Everything flourishes, even at the end of the season. Each gardener has only one raised bed and so the space is treasured and abundant. I imagine the competition for 'Best Gardener' is fierce!

Bostall Community Gardens is a huge tribute to the people who started the project in 2014 when the space was a rubbish dump, although it had once been a small plant nursery, belonging to the council, which closed in the 1980s.

It is also a tribute to those who continue to maintain the gardens in such wonderful condition and a lesson to all of us. We don't always need to turn to the council or the government — we can do it for ourselves. I feel privileged to have found this site.

Access: Viola Avenue SE2 0TQ
Opening times: Open to visitors Fridays 12.00 pm to 2.00 pm
Designation: Community Garden
Friends of Bostall Community Garden: www.facebook.com

Path into the gardens

Bostall Heath & Bostall Woods

Bostall Heath was one of the wastes of the Manor of Plumstead, and it is an area on the side and top of Bostall Hill. The hillside slopes steeply down to the Thames plain below, and although it was once heathland, today it is a woodland of sessile oaks, silver birch, chestnut, sycamore, beech, pine and cherry trees. Gorse and broom, bright yellow and buzzing with insects in the summer, grow in patches of grassland and amongst the clumps of heather.

57

From 1736, the Lords of the Manor were the Trustees of Queen's College, Oxford, and in 1866 they enclosed the Heath with the aim of building houses. The Courts declared this illegal, and in 1878, the Metropolitan Board of Works took over the area and built a keeper's lodge and sports facilities. Clam Field was added in 1894 as a recreation ground.

During WWII, four anti-aircraft guns stood on the hilltop heath, manned by Royal Marines.

Old Park Wood was on the estate of Sir Julian Goldsmid and overlooked the Wickham Lane Valley. The LCC bought the woods in 1892, and they are now known as Bostall Woods. Partly Ancient Woodland, they are magical.

In 1905, Lt Col J J Sexby described the Heath and woods as "the most attractive of the Kentish commons. Indeed we may go so far as to say that every other common of the Metropolis, with the possible exception of Epping Forest, must yield to them the palm of beauty. There are few places so close to the busy hum of London which have retained so sylvan a character." [43]

A beautiful beech wood crowns the top of the hill while the slopes down to the valley are covered in oaks (sessile and pedunculate), chestnut and birch trees, with ground cover of holly, hawthorn, wild roses, hazels and ivy, and there are bluebells and wild daffodils, perhaps the only native site of wild daffodils in the capital.

These facts don't tell you about the soughing of the wind in the branches, the twisted trunks of the old trees, and the tangible atmosphere, the feeling that the trees are aware of my presence as I wander among them. On the edges of the woods, away from the well-used main paths, the old trees feel as though they are protecting me, but it is perhaps wise to have company in these lonely corners.

Access: Bostall Hill and Longleigh Lane SE2 0RB
Opening times: Always open
Facilities: Car park, outdoor gym, cricket nets, bowling green, benches, toilets
Designation: SINC of Metropolitan Importance, part SSSI, Public Park, Common and Heath, on the Green Chain Walk
Size: c.78 hectares in Greenwich (not including Clam Field) (193 acres)
Friends of Bostall Heath and Woods: www.facebook.com

Bostall Woods in November

The beech trees in Bostall Woods in winter

Above and below: *Bostall Heath and Clam Field*
Opposite: *Bostall Heath on the hillside north of Bostall Hill, and now woodland*

Plumstead Cemetery

58

"A cemetery should sooth sorrow, as well as call forth profitable reflection," says Old Humphrey,[44] and this beautiful site, with its views over woods and hills, is just such a place. Plumstead Cemetery opened in 1890 on a sloping hillside, a "quietly spectacular location"[45] which was once Old Park Farm.

In the southern corner, glorious ash trees glow in soft autumn light, offset by dark–leaved mature conifers. The terraces nearby are both acid and base–rich grassland; the latter indicates limestone and we know chalk was quarried in Wickham Lane below the cemetery. Both support a wide variety of wildflowers including wild allium, Star of Bethlehem, buttercups and various grasses.

A secret little path along the wall on Cemetery Lane is crowded with blubells in spring. The gravestones rest quietly here, under old trees, and it is calm, peaceful and very beautiful.

In the 1880s, the railways were expanding into South East London, the dockyards and the Royal Arsenal were increasingly busy and the population was rising. The Parish Church of St Nicholas had closed its churchyard to burials in 1855, and the extended graveyard was also nearly full.

In 1888, the Chairman of the Burial Board in Woolwich, Mr E T Smith, asked the vestry to sanction a loan of £7,000 to buy a "most convenient and suitable spot for their burial ground, picturesquely placed between Wickham Lane and the wooded heights of Bostall Heath, a site easily easily accessible from the town, and beautiful to look upon."[46] This was Plumstead Cemetery.

Two recipients of the Victoria Cross are buried here: Private Thomas Flawn for action during the Basuto War in South Africa in 1879; and Gunner Alfred Smith in 1885 for action during the battle of Abu Klea in the Nile Expeditionary Campaign to relieve General Gordon. The Victoria Cross is awarded for "most conspicuous bravery, or some daring or pre–eminent act of valour or self–sacrifice, or extreme devotion to duty in the presence of the enemy."[47] Only 1,358 VCs have been awarded since it was created in 1854.

The cemetery has 187 war graves: 106 from WWI and eighty–one from WWII. There are also a number of graves with memorials to people killed in the Boer War of 1899–1902. A small group of stones near Lodge Lane gate remembers women and children killed in WWII, and a pink granite obelisk remembers workers killed in an explosion at the Arsenal in 1903.

Access: Cemetery Road SE2 0NS
Opening times: 9.00 am to dusk, but check website
Facilities: Chapel, toilets, benches
Designation: Cemetery, SINC of Borough Importance Grade II
Size: 12 hectares (30 acres)

Plumstead Common

59

Queen's College Oxford owned Plumstead Common and in 1850 started enclosing the land and laying down new roads prior to building upmarket houses. They also gave the military, based in Woolwich, permission to use the ground for manoeuvres with horses and gun carriages. This destroyed the vegetation on the site and made the area unusable for local people. Then the college proposed a permanent lease to the military.

But the quiet, rural plateau in north west Kent was ancient common land and by 1876 local people were very angry indeed.

In July 1876, John de Morgan addressed a crowd outside the Old Mill pub on the common. He was an activist in the Commons Protection League which wanted to maintain these areas for public use. Thousands of angry people marched to the site and took down fencing. The government feared the rioting would spread, arrested de Morgan and rapidly passed the Plumstead Common Act of 1878 which ensured that about one hundred acres of land remained as public open space in perpetuity.

The London Metropolitan Council bought the Common in 1877, and the London Borough of Greenwich took over management in 1965.

The Common is a flat plateau over a mile long, with steep ravines leading down to the former marshes below. It is composed of the Blackheath Beds, a layer of mainly black flint pebbles in sand, with some layers of shell, on top of chalk and clay. They were laid down 65–25 million years ago and were once beneath the sea. The Blackheath Beds are exposed at the top of The Slade and in Gilbert's Pit in Maryon Park. The Dog Rocks or Puddingstone Rocks near the entrance to the adventure playground are cemented Blackheath Beds material and the largest outcrop outside Hertfordshire.

The Plumstead Pantry

As late as the 1870s, the land between the Common and what was to become Shrewsbury Park was farmland, and Plum Lane was a country lane.

Somehow, the Common maintains a countryside atmosphere and is a lovely place for a long walk to blow away the cobwebs.

Plumstead Common West

Warwick Terrace and the small complex of buildings which include the Old Mill and The Plumstead Pantry are roughly in the middle of the Common. To the west is a park with the Plumstead Common Bowling Club, tennis courts and dog walking area, an adventure playground for children, which replaced an Edwardian bandstand, and a nature conservation area.

The original mill was built in the 17th century; today's Old Mill dates from 1764 and it was still grinding wheat for local housewives in the early 1800s. Around the mid–1800s, it turned to making beer but brewing ended in the 1960s. The body of the mill is joined to the Old Mill pub.

Plumstead Common Nature Conservation Area

This deep ravine on the side of Plumstead Common is also known as Bird's Nest Hollow and the Dip. It was originally on the Bramblebury estate and is shown on the OS Map of 1873.

Like many bare sites, it was a rubbish tip until the residents of Blendon Terrace took action. They founded the Plumstead Common Environment Group (now the Friends of Plumstead Common) and persuaded the council to create a nature conservation area. In 2004 the reserve of 0.5 hectares (1.25 acres) was designated a SINC of Local Importance. What a tremendous achievement!

Sycamore is gradually being coppiced and thinned amongst the ash and oak trees. Sessile oaks are the dominant species with a thick undergrowth of holly, hawthorn, ivy, hazel and elder. There is a single, very old black mulberry tree and bluebells flower in the spring.

Do visit this pretty, secret and wooded hollow to which easiest access is from Vicarage Park SE18 7SU.

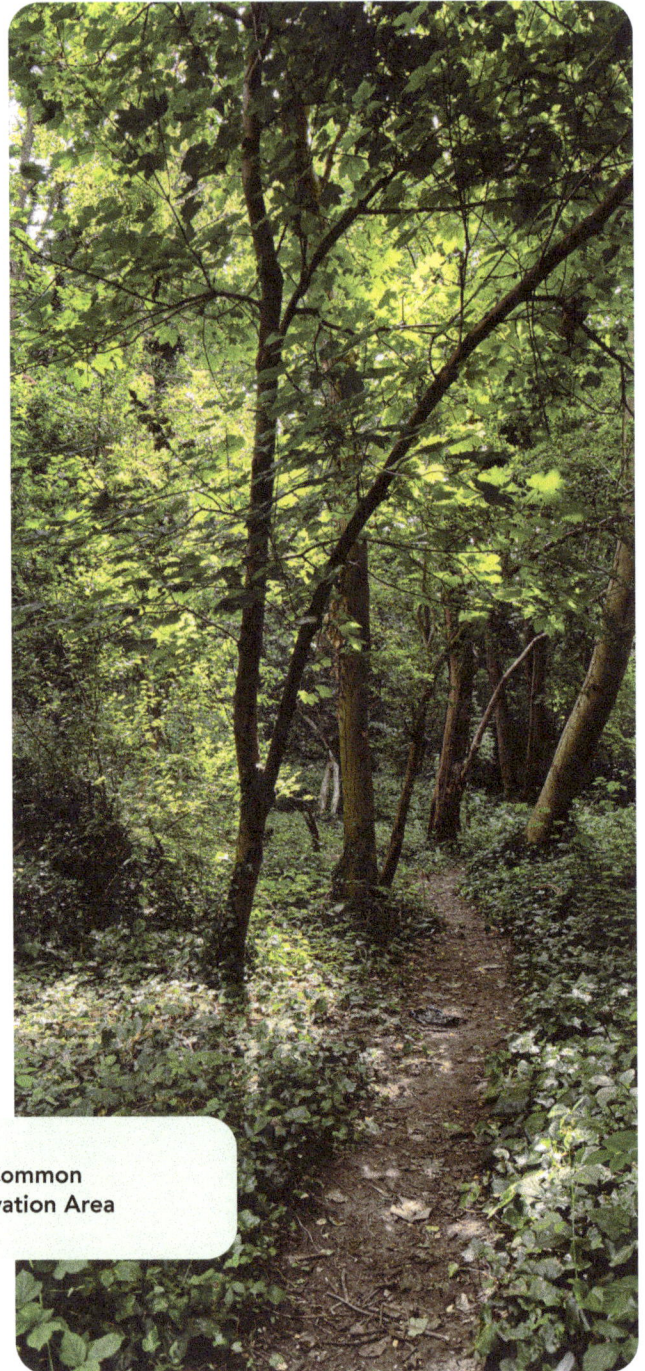

Plumstead Common
Nature Conservation Area

Plumstead Common East

The Slade

If you haven't found The Slade before you will be surprised! It is one of the ravines off the plateau of Plumstead Common. In the 1870s, this area and the land to the north between Piedmont and Lakedale Roads was The Park, "a charming spot, thickly wooded, and having a stream and miniature cascades."[48]

The lake is a natural pond fed by a stream running down from Shrewsbury Park, which was culverted in the 1880s. It takes storm water and prevents flooding in Roydene Road.

The sides of the ravine are covered in gorse and wildflowers, and the trees have matured over the years — London plane trees, birches, poplars, oaks and willow trees crowd round the water. A major restoration project in the 1990s created a biodiverse and clean site which attracts a variety of wildlife. The site is owned by Thames Water.

Winn's Common

At first sight, Winn's Common is a flat, bare expanse of grass on top of a plateau. Then you notice a mound in the middle, a Bronze Age Tumulus which is a scheduled monument on the Register of Historic England. It is known as a bowl barrow and probably dates from 2400–1500 BC, suggesting very early settlement here.

Winn's Common is named after Thomas Winn, a local landowner who built almshouses on the common for poor widows. They were later replaced with a workhouse. He died in 1800 and is buried in the Church of St Nicholas.

A lake is shown as early as 1867; by 1900 this was a boating lake which was damaged during WWII and after that was changed to a paddling pool in the adventure playground.

During WWII, a barrage balloon unit from RAF Kidbrooke was stationed here. Barrage balloons could raise a steel net to 5,000 feet to deter dive bombers flying below that height. After the war, 143 prefabs were erected on Winn's Common to house people made homeless by the war. Each home had a small garden, kitchen and bathroom, and they were finally removed c.1957–58. People who lived here report many happy memories of their time in the area.

Workhouse Woods

These woods are in another small ravine on the common, between Lakedale and Riverdale Roads. This small but beautiful area has been recovered by the Friends of Plumstead Common with funding from Tesco's Bags of Help fund and the Postcode Lottery.

The Workhouse was built in 1870 on Plumstead High Street between Riverdale Road (previously Skittle Lane) and Tewson Road. Its land extended towards the common to include an orchard and a piggery. In 1930, the workhouse system ended and the London County Council (LCC) took control of the site. The buildings were finally demolished in 1992 and replaced with housing, but the area of the orchard was reprieved, and, today, it is Workhouse Woods.

In the woods there are field maples, a Monterey pine, and a very old oak tree with the usual undergrowth of ivy and holly. The plateau in this northerly section of the common is rough, with lots of gorse, and acid grassland with common bent–grass, red fescue, yellow cat's ear and sheep's sorrel. The sycamore, pedunculate oak and birches are secondary woodland. This is perhaps what Plumstead Common looked like, once upon a time.

Great Bartletts

The steep hillside in the far east of Winns Common down to Wickham Lane is 1.5 hectares (3.8 acres) of woodland, mainly native trees but also Swedish whitebeam and red horse chestnut. The Green Chain Walk runs through the woods.

Access: Plumstead Common Road SE18 2RT
Opening times: Always open
Facilities: Benches, sports grounds, children's playgrounds, tennis courts, bowling green, café, pub
Designation: Public Open Space, Winn's Common, Bleak Hill & The Slade are SINCs of Borough Importance Grade I
Size: 30 hectares (74 acres)
Friends of Plumstead Common: http://plumcomfriends.org

59b,
59c,
59d,
59e

59b

The Slade in late March

Winn's Common and Bleak Hill Lane in late October

59c

Dipping down into
Workhouse Woods in late October

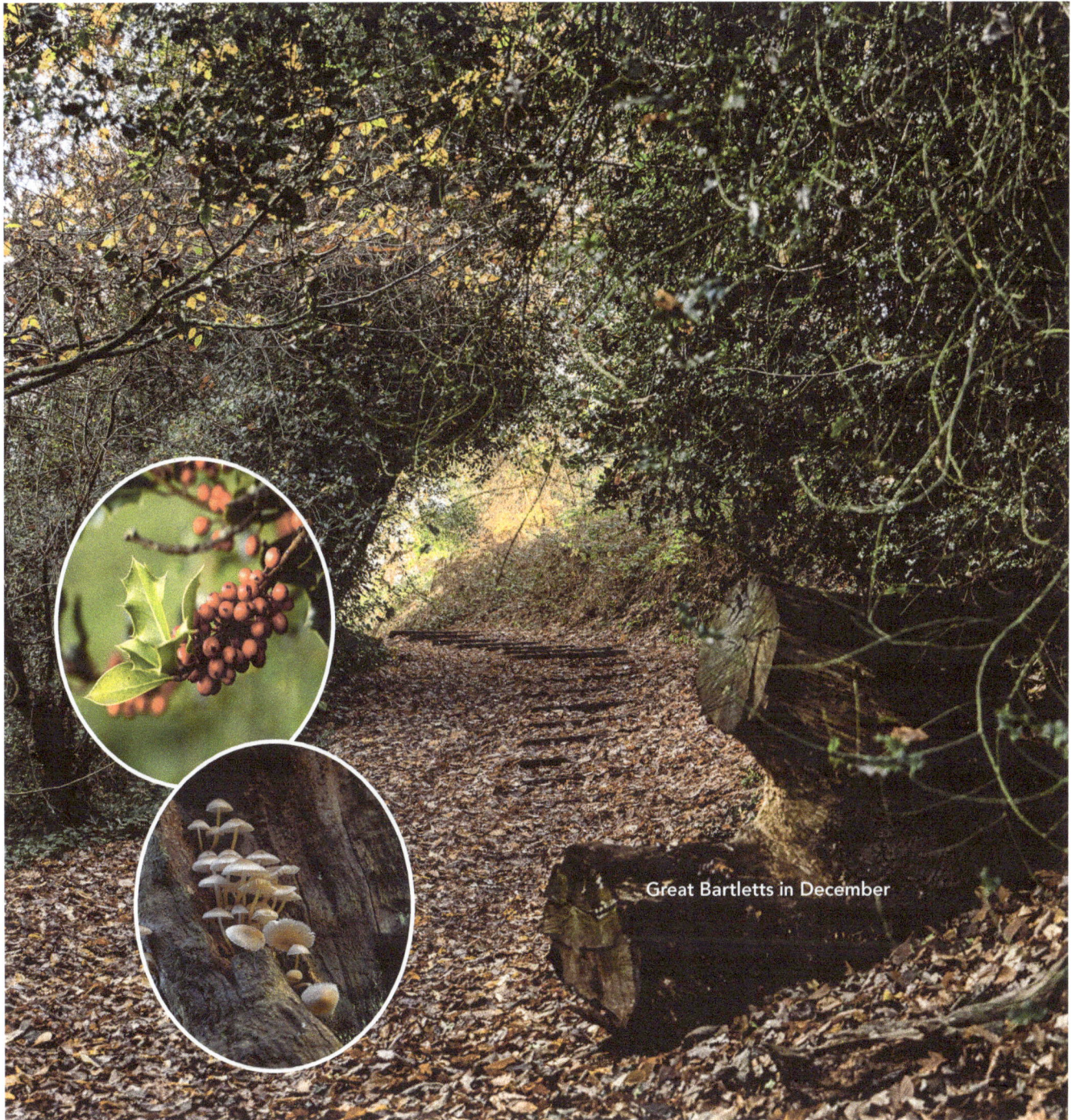

Great Bartletts in December

Plumstead Gardens

Plumstead Gardens is a delightful surprise, a welcome expanse of green which hides away in bare streets of unvaried housing.

At the end of the 19th century, the area was fields, possibly part of Manor House Farm, and by 1914, the site was allotments. The gates carry the crest of the Metropolitan Borough of Woolwich which created the park after WWII.

60

The OS map of 1957 shows a design in two halves: the eastern end was laid out as an ornamental garden with a raised terrace on Church Manor Way, a pond with a footbridge in a sunken garden on the central axis, rose beds, and trees or shrubs around the boundaries. In the western half there was a children's playground, a paddling pool and a roller skating rink.

Today the park is still in two halves, but there are several changes. The children's playground is enlarged, there is no paddling pool and the roller skating rink is a raised platform. Multipurpose ball courts and table tennis tables have been added.

The formal gardens were removed in the 1990s, and the pond was filled in. Two mature gingko biloba trees stand proudly on the raised terrace, and mature willows, birches, ash trees and sycamores line the boundaries.

The terrace could be enhanced with colourful, carefully pruned shrubs, and while the sunken garden is surrounded by a thin border of wildflowers, wouldn't it be wonderful if the entire sunken area was wild flowers? It would look like a large bouquet, 'tied' with a neat and pretty low brick wall.

The new Friends have already made a difference, and are determined on rejuvenating the park. They deserve support.

Access: Church Manorway SE18 1EL
Opening times: 9.00 am to dusk
Facilities: Multipurpose ball courts, all–weather cricket net, table tennis tables, children's playground, seats
Designation: Public Park
Size: 2.5 hectares (6 acres)
Friends of Plumstead Gardens: www.facebook.com

Corn Cockle

Above: *The western end of the park with sports facilities and childrens' playground*
Below: *The former formal garden with a hint of the sunken garden on the left*

Rockliffe Gardens

From the 1860s, the Wickham Lane Brickworks, which consisted of the Cemetery Brickyard, the South Metropolitan Brickyard and Gregory's Pit (aka Wickham Lane Brick Pit), covered the area from the boundary of Woolwich Old Cemetery, along the west of Wickham Lane to Bournewood Road.

And immediately opposite the brickworks were chalk pits. There were three chalk pits in this area: Cemetery Mine, South Metropolitan Mine and one other. Apparently there were up to two miles of underground passages and chambers in the mines, and shafts as deep as 150 feet.

The brickworks mixed clay and sand from Upnor, Woolwich and Thanet Formations from their open pits with chalk from their own underground mines but also exploited local brickearth.

Chalk was used to make cement but a small percentage, added to the clay, c.15%, produced bricks with a yellow colour.

Woolwich Borough Council bought the site of the Cemetery Brickyard in 1935, and the Borough Engineer, H W Tee, laid out an ornamental garden which was opened by the Mayor of Woolwich, Miss M Crout, in 1937.

However, in the same year, the ground collapsed and holes opened on the Rockliffe Gardens site. There was another collapse in 1938, and in 1939 a workman died while the council was filling in the boreholes of the mines. The Woolwich Subsidences Act was passed by Parliament in 1950 enabling the council to do whatever was necessary to secure the safety of the area. The underground mines were filled with fly–ash slurry and sealed off, and this stabilised the ground.

The gardens gradually fell into disrepair until a Friends Group formed in 2008 to regenerate the park.

Below: Rockliffe Gardens in early May

61

Recently, the council has installed new park furniture and restored the wildlife pond, which is overlooked by bare terracing, waiting patiently for plants.

Swathes of cow parsley and bluebells cling to the hillside below the ornamental pond, but they are in danger because the paths are spreading. This is a magical area of bluebells, something rarely found in RBG, and deadhedging would afford easy protection.

The gardens lie between Woolwich old and new cemeteries and are easily overlooked, but do take time to visit as they are surprisingly beautiful, particularly in the spring.

Access: Radnor Crescent, SE18 Camdale Road,SE18 2DS
Opening times: 9.00 am to dusk
Facilities: Benches
Designation: Public Park, SINC of Borough Importance Grade II
Size: 2 hectares (5 acres)
Friends of Rockliffe Gardens: https://rockliffegardens.weebly.com

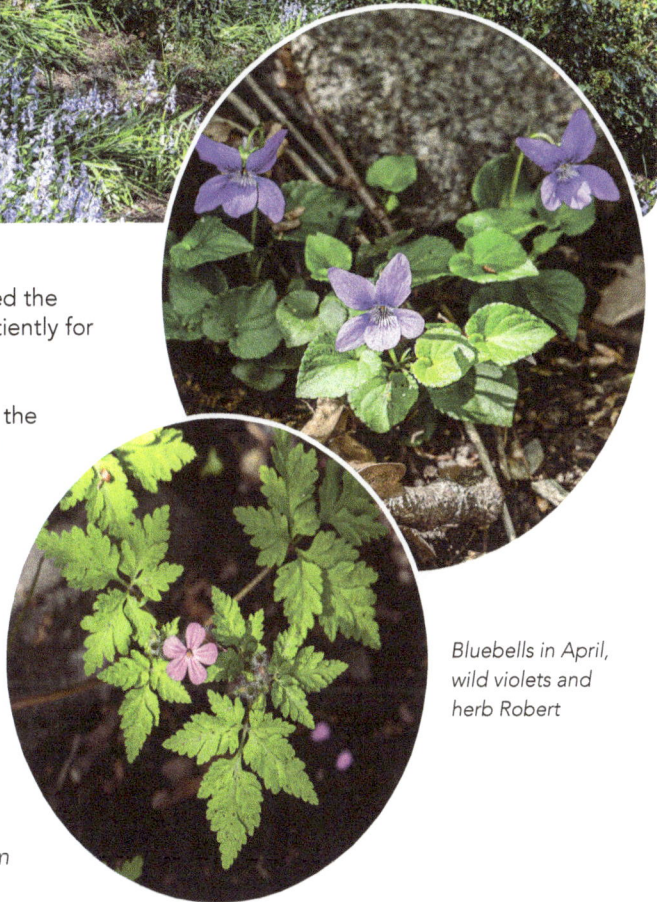

Bluebells in April, wild violets and herb Robert

St Nicholas Churchyard & Gardens

One thousand years ago, St Nicholas stood on a spur of chalky ground which lifted the building above the marshes. Just yards to the north lay the original road across the marshes, today's Blithdale Road.

St Nicholas was the patron saint of various groups of people, including sailors, and as Plumstead was a fishing and farming community, that perhaps explains the dedication of the church. The church in Deptford, once also a fishing village, is similarly dedicated to the saint.

It is remarkable that the building has endured. Today's south aisle was the original nave, the west wall is 12th century, the south aisle is 13th century, like the

62

St Nicholas Church, Plumstead

transcept, and the north aisle was added in the 15th century and is the present nave. By the 1600s, the church was in disrepair, and John Gossage, a wealthy local farmer, stepped in and paid for the rebuilding and the rather incongruous tower of 1662–64. Somehow the church was in ruins again by the 1800s, with trees growing in the aisles! C H Cooke undertook restorations in 1867–68.

But, in 1907, the church was damaged again by huge explosions in two gunpowder magazines between Woolwich and Erith. Greenaway and Newberry undertook repairs and enlargements on the north side in 1907–08. The south transcept and the Lady Chapel suffered bomb damage in WWII but were not replaced when the building was repaired in 1959. The church is now Grade II* listed.

Burials in the churchyard of St Nicholas stopped in 1855, but by the 1880s, even the enlarged graveyard was full because Plumstead was expanding so rapidly. The new Plumstead Cemetery opened in Wickham Lane in 1890.

The extended burial ground is St Nicholas Gardens, on a sloping site next to the High Street. A diagonal path crosses the grass amongst randomly growing mature trees, and a few gravestones line the perimeter of the gardens. They seem like forgotten slabs of stone rather than memorials to people who once lived here.

"There are few spots in England more peaceful, and more hallowed than our village churchyards when they are treated with the reverance which is their due" wrote Isabella Holmes in 1896, but sadly the "somewhat rural flavour" of St Nicholas has gone.[49]

Access: St Nicholas Road SE18 1HJ
Opening times: Gardens always open; for church, see the website
Facilities: Seats
Designation: Church and Public Park
Size: 1.2 hectares (3 acres)
Friends of St Nicholas Gardens: http://plumcomfriends.org/

St Nicholas Gardens

Corners in Plumstead & Abbey Woods

Abbey Wood Park SE2 9PG

Abbey Wood Park is three separate green spaces, mainly grassed and with mature trees. The western park, separated by housing and a school, has sports facilities, a Grade II listed sculpture, 'Delight' 1962–67 by A H Gerrard, and a car park. This Public Park of 4.8 hectares (12 acres) is always open.

Villas Road Playground SE18 7PW

The OS map of 1870 shows this as a brick field and clay mill; by 1896 the area was filled with housing. Today's tower blocks date from the 1960s so this may be the date of the playground as well. This small park is always open

63a
63b

Abbey Wood Park

Villas Road Playground

William Barefoot Gardens

William Barefoot Gardens, originally part of the Wickham Lane Brickworks complex, was landscaped as a park and opened in 1942. It is pretty in the springtime when the bluebells appear.

But, as you walk through the gates at other times of the year, the rocky terraces which greet you are depressingly bare. Yet they could be planted with ferns, bergenias, geraniums, Japanese anemones, liriope, anamanthele. This small, quiet park could be so attractive...

William Barefoot (1872-1941) was a local Councillor in Eltham and three times Mayor of Woolwich who served on the National Executive of the Labour Party. He is also remembered in Well Hall Pleasaunce and William Barefoot Drive in the Coldharbour Estate.

There are benches on the grass and the park is open from 9 am to dusk.

Access: Alliance Road, SE18 2BA
Designation: Public Park
Size: 0.3 hectares (0.7 acres)

63c

Woolwich Old Cemetery

The original Woolwich Cemetery hugs the hillside opposite Bostall Woods, glorious and peaceful parkland.

"I would not say that a converted graveyard is a better garden than a converted square, but yet there is something more interesting about it — it is so very human."[50]

One senses that those who were buried here rest peacefully

The cemetery was laid out in 1856 by the Woolwich Burial Board on the edge of Plumstead Common to replace the graveyard of St Mary Magdalene, Woolwich, which closed the previous year. Within thirty years, it too was full, replaced by Woolwich New Cemetery. The original Anglican chapel remains, but a second, non-denominational chapel has been demolished, as has the original lodge. Many of the gravestones have been cleared from the main body of the cemetery, and some are leaning against the south east wall.

But this is more than a park, and of course there is sadness.

On 3 September 1878, the Princess Alice steamer was returning from Sheerness in Kent with 700 passengers on board. Just after rounding Tripcock Point, she took the wrong sailing lane along Gallions Reach and collided with the coal steamer Bywell Castle at the point where raw sewage had just been released into the Thames. The steamer broke into three and 631 people died. There was a public appeal for a memorial which was erected in May 1880 and 120 victims are buried here.

A small CWGC site stands in the south east corner of the cemetery, and other Kipling stones are dotted about. John Taylor VC (1822–1857) was in the naval brigade which took part in the siege of Sebastopol in 1854–55 and has a striking black gravestone. He was decorated posthumously in 1857 for helping a wounded colleague in battle; two of his colleagues were similarly decorated.

64

The beautiful old trees give solace here, stately, majestic, enduring, and green even in the extreme summer of 2022. Scots pine trees line two walls, there is an avenue of cedar trees, copper beeches are mature and elegant, and lime trees stand gracefully around the grounds with slender birch trees. Wildflowers flourish in the grass.

This is a comforting place.

Access: Kings Highway SE18 2BL
Opening times: 9.00 am until dusk, check website
Facilities: Chapel, toilets, benches
Designation: Cemetery, SINC of Borough Importance Grade II
Size: 13 hectares (32 acres)

Both photographs:
Woolwich Old Cemetery in Autumn

Woolwich New Cemetery

65

Woolwich New Cemetery opened in 1885 to the south east of the old cemetery. As you walk through the gates and past the WWI memorial, the outlook is rather bleak. The graves are laid out in straight lines with hardly any trees to soften the landscape. The reality of life, and death, is laid out in front of you and has to be confronted.

But walk towards the far end and the site changes. William Barefoot Gardens is on the slope below the cemetery and the north eastern boundary was in Bourne Spring Wood, according to the OS map published in 1870. Mature trees give shelter, the ground slopes and graves are less regularly placed.

As always there are war graves. The two Woolwich cemeteries together have 179 war graves, which are marked with Kipling stones. Thomas Monaghan (1833–95) was a trumpeter in the Second Dragoon Guards and he was just twenty–five when he was awarded the VC in 1858 for conspicuous bravery in action in India.

And there is a shared grave for five men killed in an explosion at Woolwich Arsenal in 1939.

On this winter's day, with snow thick on the ground, I was reminded that soldiers endured temperatures of –20C on the Somme during WWI.

> They shall grow not old, as we that are left grow old:
> Age shall not weary them, nor the years condemn.
> At the going down of the sun and in the morning
> We will remember them.
> Laurence Binyon, 21.9.1914[51]

Access: Camdale Road SE18 2DS
Opening times: 9.00 am to dusk, but check the website
Facilities: Chapel, seats
Designation: SINC of Borough Importance Grade II, Cemetery
Size: 8 hectares (20 acres)

SHOOTERS HILL PARKS & WOODLANDS

The largest group of woods and meadows in the Borough of Greenwich are on Shooters Hill, and much of the area is Ancient Woodland. This means the area has existed as woodland for at least 400 years and been relatively undisturbed. Come here to linger, slow down, find peace...

The woods on Shooters Hill were in the Manor of Eltham and owned by the Crown. Over the centuries, the woods were used for hunting, but also managed for income. Hornbeam and oak were burned to make charcoal for fuel; oak bark produced tannins for tanning leather in the extensive industries in Bermondsey; oak was used for shipbuilding in the Deptford and other shipyards along the Thames; and the trees were coppiced for various purposes including tool handles, stakes and firewood.

A Roman road, Watling Street, crosses the hill, and in around 1800, nearly fifty coaches a day used this as the main route between London and Dover. It was a dangerous road, frequented by highwaymen who were not deterred by the sight of bodies swinging on the gallows at the bottom of the hill.

Shooters Hill rises to 132 metres (433 feet) and is a prominent landmark. It was the site of a beacon in the 16th century and a semaphore station stood there in the 18th century, on the line from the Admiralty in Central London to Deal. During WWII, anti-aircraft guns were placed on top of the hill. Today it remains easily visible from miles around.

Lady James was probably given permission by the Crown Commissioners to build Severndroog Castle in 1784, a folly designed by Richard Jupp in memory of her husband. The tower was used as a surveying point in an Anglo-French survey mapping England from 1784–90 which led to the OS maps. It was then used in 1848 by the Royal Engineers when they mapped London. Severndroog Castle is a Grade II* listed building today.

In the 19th century, a few large country mansions were built on the hill, but none remain today apart from the more modest Holbrook (c.1838) at 162 Shooters Hill Road. The Bull and Red Lion are Victorian replacements for 18th century pubs and a small reminder of the 19th century.

We are lucky the woods have survived! In 1812, the Office of Woods and Forests managed the land on behalf of the Crown Commissioners but allowed the War Office use and gave the public access. In 1847, the Duke of Wellington suggested it become the Shooters Hill Necropolis and United Services Mausoleum, but the scheme was abandoned. In 1860, there was discussion about building a huge fort on the hill, but that plan was also abandoned.

The Crown Commissioners sold the woods to the LCC, in three lots, for public use, starting in 1922, and today they are protected as a Site of Special Scientific Interest (SSSI) and managed by Greenwich Borough Council.

Designation: Shooters Hill Woods, SINC of Metropolitan Importance, Local Nature Reserve since 1992, part SSSI
Size: Shooters Hill Woods, c.97 hectares (c.240 acres)

Essential reading:

Bagnold, Colonel A H, Articles on Shooters Hill from *The Parish Magazine of Christ Church, Shooters Hill*, (1936–1938, RBG Archive)

Wareham, Tom, *Oxleas; History, Conservation and Connection in a Suburban Woodland*, (2020, printed by Amazon)

Severndroog Castle

Eaglesfield Park

66

Eaglesfield Park, on the top of Shooters Hill, is the loftiest park in Greenwich and has wonderful views into Kent. The upper section is grassed, framed by mature London plane trees, some willows and hornbeams, and with a smart children's playground, which in the past was a paddling pool where children sailed their toy boats.

Sir John Lidgbird was made High Sheriff of Kent in 1741, and he lived nearby in Broom Hall, now replaced by housing at Hill End. The park probably takes its name from his coat of arms which included two eagles.

In 1907, the Woolwich Borough Council bought land here for recreational space to service the new housing in the area. Lt Col J J Sexby laid out the park, and Eaglesfield Park opened to the public in 1908.

And there is a surprise!

Woodcot was one of the grand mansions on Shooters Hill. It was built before 1745, and surrounded by gardens with a large ornamental pond fed by a spring. The house was demolished in 1875 and replaced with 1 and 2 Woodcot Cottages in Cleanthus Close, and nos. 171–181 Shooters Hill Road.

The Eaglesfield Park pond was probably the ornamental pond for Woodcot. It hides behind a belt of trees and was overgrown and neglected until a group of Friends, the council, Environmental Wildlife Charities, Groundwork UK and Froglife came together, and raised money for renovation. The delightful wildlife pond reopened in 2011, surrounded by plants which enjoy the damp, rich soil. Railings and paths in the park were upgraded at the same time.

The lower half of the park, across the road and next to Shooters Hill Golf Club, is managed as open meadow, surrounded by a belt of trees. Blackberries are abundant here in late summer!

Do visit this charming park at any time of the year.

Access: Eaglesfield Road SE18 3BX
Opening times: Always open
Facilities: Children's play area, picnic area, benches
Designation: Green Flag Public Park, on Green Chain Walk
Size: 3.65 hectares (9 acres)
Friends of Eaglesfield Park: https://eaglesfieldpark.org

Above: Lily pond with yellow loosestrife
Below: Blackberries in the meadow in the lower park in late summer

Shrewsbury Park & Tumulus

67

The Earls of Shrewsbury built Shrewsbury House in 1789 on their estates at Shooters Hill. Soon after, the property was acquired by George IV and thereafter had various owners.

In 1908, the LCC bought nine acres of the grounds to make Eaglesfield Park. In 1916, Fred Halse bought the house and the southern part of the grounds, demolished the mansion and built the current Shrewsbury House. Today it is a library and community centre, and situated further to the south than the original Shrewsbury House. In 1928, the LCC bought the northern part of the estate for Shrewsbury Park.

During WWII, a barrage balloon was situated in today's car park. It was manned by the 901 Barrage Balloon Squadron which was based at RAF Kidbrooke.

The park has several distinct areas, and they are all enjoyable.

A grassy meadow lies on top of the hill, with far-reaching views northwards to the Thames and Essex. The grass here is managed as meadow and cut every eight weeks to allow the wildflowers to grow and seed. Below the meadow is Dot Hill Road, an old lane which runs through the park, and beyond that is a dense area of young secondary woodland, Dot Hill Community Woodland, 5.4 hectares (13.4 acres) of oaks, hawthorn, willow and cherries. And along Plum Lane is a triangle of meadow, with views towards the City this time.

But the real joy is the magic of the Ancient Woodland, High Grove, alongside Plum Lane.

As I step through the perimeter trees guarding the wood, I leave London behind and enter a world of calm amongst the oak and beech trees, birch and hornbeams. It is as if I was in a sanctuary. The only sounds are the ring-necked parakeets in the treetops, and the squirrels.

Sadly, there are large areas of bare ground which are very muddy in the winter; would the woods benefit from deadhedging to allow the undergrowth to return?

Above: *An oak moot in Ancient Woodland in Shrewsbury Park*
Below: *Meadows along Plum Lane*

Shrewsbury Park

Access to Shrewsbury Park:
Plum Lane SE18 3AG
Opening times: Check website
Facilities: Benches, car park
Designation: SINC of Borough
Importance Grade I, Green
Chain Walk crosses the park
Size: 14.4 hectares (36 acres)
Friends of Shrewsbury Park:
www.fspark.org.uk

Mayplace Lane

Mayplace Lane was an old track which led up from the marshes, perhaps up Sandy Hill Road, to the tumulus on Shrewsbury Lane and on to Shooters Hill. Did it connect with Stoney Alley?

Above: *Mayplace Lane SE18 3BP*
Below: *Shrewsbury Tumulus SE18 3BP*

Shrewsbury Tumulus

The Shrewsbury Tumulus stands just outside the park on a grassy mound enclosed by railings. It was one of several Bronze Age burial mounds on Shooters Hill, but this is the only one which remains.

Up until c.1860, the site was a large open space known as The Furze Field and a favourite picnic spot. The other tumuli were destroyed in the 1930s during the construction of houses. The sites of the tumuli were all listed by Col A H Bagnold.

The Shrewsbury Tunulus covers 0.07 hectares (0.2 acres) and it is permanently closed to the public. It stands at the entrance to Mayplace Lane SE18 3BP

Woodlands Farm

Between 1800 and 1830, a dense forest called Bushy Lees Wood was cleared to establish Woodlands Farm. The farm was originally 49 hectares (122 acres) and grew wheat, vegetables, fruit and oats to supply shops in Plumstead, Woolwich and even London. A trace horse was added to wagons to get the produce up Shooters Hill, and apparently it was quite common for travellers or traders to stop at the farm and ask for a trace horse to be pulled up the hill. In 1920, the Baldock family sold the farm to the RACS (Royal Arsenal Co-operative Society) and moved to their second farm at Cliffe.

The RACS farmed pigs for pork and bacon, barley and hay. An abattoir was opened on the farm but closed in the late 1980s and farming ended. Local people came together to raise money and set up the trust in 1997 to save the site from housing development.

Woodlands Farm Trust continues as a working farm, with a variety of rare breed animals and lambing in the spring. There are no artificial fertilisers on the farm, and hay is cut once a year. As a result, wildflowers, insects, butterflies and birds are thriving, and the farm produces honey.

The orchards offer fruit picking in the autumn. Field boundaries are hedges, and the traditional skill of hedgelaying is practised and taught. The farm has an education area where children are encouraged to learn about growing food. It is the largest community farm in London.

The Plumstead River, the River Wogebourne, runs through the farm, and through Clothworkers Wood to the north. The woods are designated wet woodlands, a rare habitat in London and in the UK.

A delightful community asset — do visit.

Access: Shooters Hill Road DA16 3RP
Opening times: Tuesday to Sunday, 9.30 am to 4.30 pm
Facilities: Farm shop, toilets, limited parking
Designation: Community Farm, SINC of Borough Importance Grade I
Size: 36 hectares (89 acres)
Woodlands Farm Trust:
http://www.thewoodlandsfarmtrust.org

68

The Cottage Garden

210

The farms and some of the animals

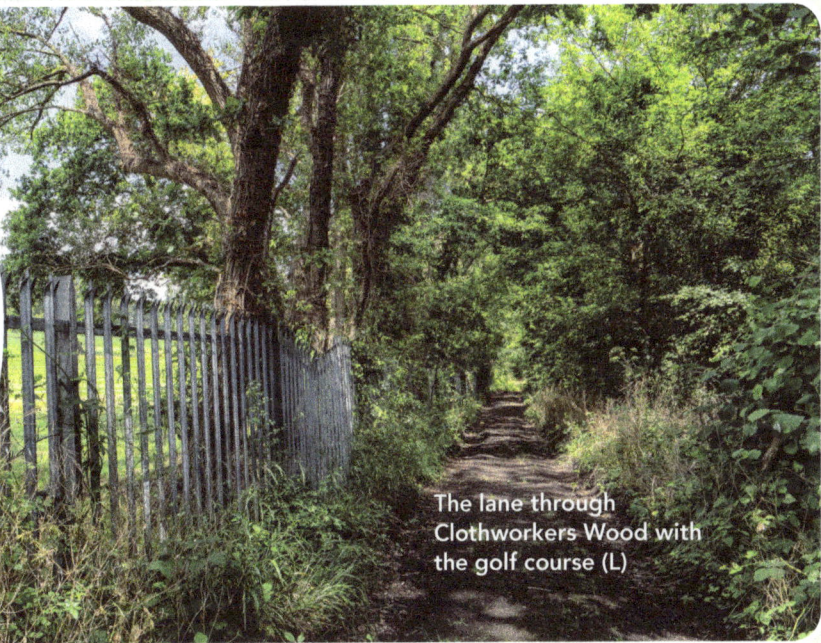
The lane through Clothworkers Wood with the golf course (L)

Eltham Common

Eltham Common is common land, and it is in two parts: the triangle of grassy meadow bounded by Shooters Hill Road and Well Hall Road, and the woodlands further up the hill. A gallows once stood at the junction of Well Hall Road and Shooters Hill; then a police station was built here in 1829. Now, the building has been converted to housing.

These are magical woods where you can slip into a different layer of time and experience, expand and sharpen your sense of being. The trees surround and welcome you, and I find it relaxing to walk here. There are rough–barked oaks and beeches, silver birches and ash trees. The undergrowth is hawthorn, hazel, holly, bramble and some gorse. And in spring you can find wood anemones and some bluebells. Unlike other areas of Shooters Hill, the trees here are secondary woodland, but even so, they communicate with you.

The open meadow is covered with flowering grasses and various wildflowers in the summer, and it is a delight to walk along the mown paths.

Over the years the land has been threatened.

The War Office built the Herbert Hospital in the 1860s and encroached on the Common when they excavated a reservoir to supply the hospital. The reservoir still stands behind fencing, an open green space next to the eastern edge of the Common. The War Office eyed the land again at the end of the 1800s when the Boer War was imminent, because the military establishment in Woolwich needed open ground for military manoeuvres.

In the 1870s, Mr Chester Haworth obtained permission from the Eltham Vestry to extract loam (a mix of sand, soil and clay) from the common but stopped when he thought he might be prosecuted for contravening common law!

The Eltham Vestry was a committee of local ratepayers, chaired by the local vicar. It was effectively the local Parochial Parish Council but with much wider responsibilities. The Vestry was responsible for protecting the rights of local people to graze their animals on the Common and harvest firewood.

Eventually it was the military which complained about the desecration of the Common. Today the area is protected.

Access: Well Hall Road SE9 6UA and car park at Severndroog Castle SE18 3RR
Opening times: Always open
Facilities: None; the Capital Ring crosses the woods and meadow.
Designation: SINC of Borough Importance Grade I
Size: c.13.2 hectares (33 acres)
Friends Group: https://www.oxleaswoodlands.uk

The woods in winter

Hazelwood Fields

Castle Wood

The wood is named after Severndroog Castle, the folly built by Lady James. A small lane leads from Shooters Hill Road to a car park from where a path leads to the Castle.

Castle Wood House was situated on the hill below the Castle, and from the car park, another tarmacked path winds round the hillside to the site.

Thomas Jackson, who owned Eltham Park, leased additional land from the Crown Estate and built Castle Wood House c.1869. Canine Cottage (previously known as Rose Cottage) to the east of the main house was either the former stable block for Castle Wood House or a lodge for the house, depending on the source of information.

Probyn Godson was the last owner, and when he died in 1920, the estate was offered for sale. Money was raised, the LCC bought the property, demolished the house and opened a public park in 1925.

The site of the house is now a flat terrace of lawn and rose beds, with a giant mature redwood tree. To the west are

woodlands, and on the hillside below the terraces is a large meadow surrounded by trees and with far-reaching views. At the bottom of the meadow, Mr Godson had a bathing pool, and the rectangular outline is still visible on aerial photographs.

In Castle Wood you can find pedunculate and sessile oaks, beeches, birches, hornbeams, chestnuts and holly trees. Stoney Alley marks the boundary with Jack Wood. The name is probably derived from the gravel and pebbles which top the hill. Under that are layers of porous clay which release springs and streams.

Hazelwood Fields

Thomas Lingham acquired the lease of Hazelwood House (c.1773) on Shooters Hill Road in the early 1800s and rebuilt it shortly after. He then acquired more land, Hazelwood Fields.

A path curves to the left of Severndroog Castle, and further up the hillside, almost hidden away, are Hazelwood Fields which are also known as Hospital Fields. Lingham built Castle House in the fields in 1829 (now a car park next to

The meadows below the former
Castle Wood House

the Memorial Hospital). Castle House Lodge still stands at the entrance of the lane from Shooters Hill Road to the Severndroog car park, but it is being modernised and will eventually be unrecognisable.

In 1883, Samuel Phillips of Holbrook House bought the lease of Castle House, and a few years later also bought Hazelwood House. His son Charles inherited the vast estate. After WWI he sold Telegraph Field, once the site of the Admiralty semaphore station, for the Memorial Hospital.

The fields are hidden and quite tricky to access, but they are also open, and quiet. And in the summer there is a colourful bank of rosebay willowherb.

Access: Rochester Way SE9 2RE or Welling Way DA16 2RP
Opening times: Always open
Facilities: Car park, café in Severndroog Castle, benches
Designation: Public Amenity Space, SINC of Metropolitan Importance
Size: c.13.5 hectares (c.33 acres)

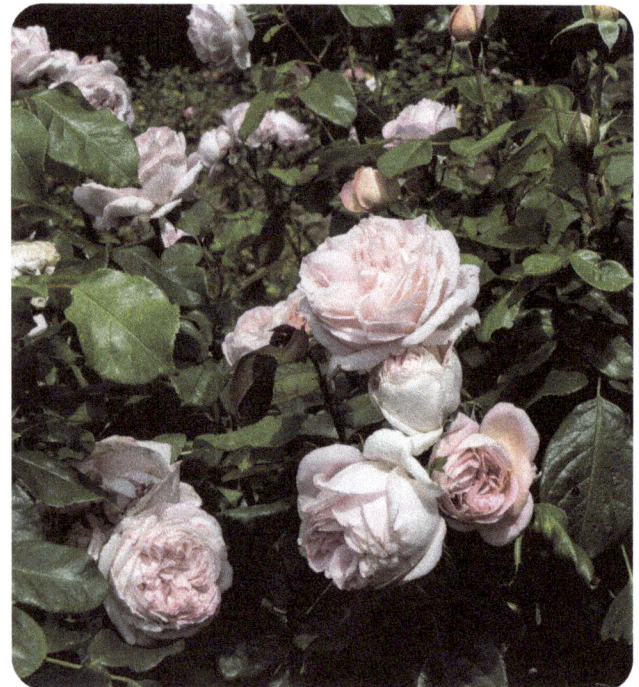

Above: The view from the site of Castle Wood House
Right: Roses on the terrace

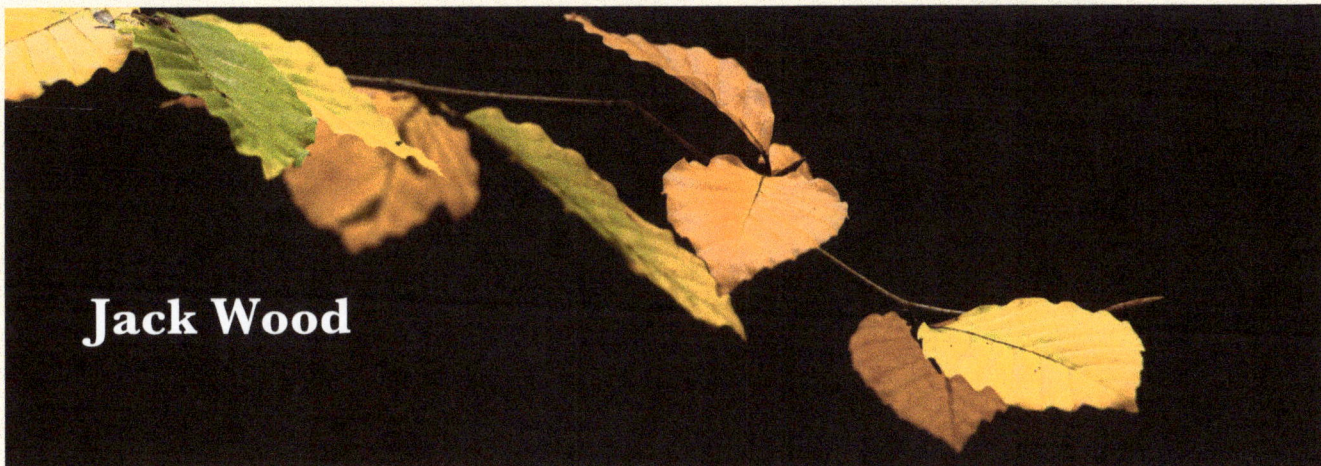

Jack Wood

Jack Wood is perhaps the most private wood on the hill. The triangular section of woods is bounded on the west by Stoney Alley, and on the east Crown Woods Lane leads to the Oxleas Wood car park.

Stoney Alley is possibly a mediaeval lane over Shooters Hill, linking Woolwich on the Thames with Eltham. The lane crosses Shooters Hill opposite The Bull, and probably led across the fields to St John the Baptist in Eltham. The lane becomes clearer as it drops down the hill, with the wall of Hazelwood Fields on one side. Two old lamp posts still stand in the lower part of the hill, although one has fallen down near the exit on to Crookston Road.

James Wilde, Baron Penzance, leased twenty-one acres of the woods to the west of Crown Woods Lane from the Crown Estate in 1861 on a ninety–nine–year lease. Ewan Christian designed the house, originally known as Mayfield but renamed Jackwood House by 1888. The house was sited on the current rose garden, and staff were housed in the building now used by the council. The hillside below the house was landscaped with lawns, woodland walks, a stream and a pond, and there was a rose garden as Wilde was passionate about roses.

The kitchen garden and orchard on the west side of the house were accessed through a small iron gate. This is a beautiful area with benches and plaques of remembrance. It is peaceful, with two magnificent magnolias. Behind the walled terrace is the Oxleas Woods Apiary.

Wilde and his wife left in 1874 and were followed by different occupiers for a few years before the Crown Commissioners put the estate up for sale in 1888. Perhaps the most notorious owners were Nat and Maxine Goodwin, who bought the house in 1898. They were followed by others, but by 1926 the house was empty. The LCC bought the property, demolished the house but left the lodge and the coach house.

Today, the landscaping has gone and the woods have matured. Trees are mainly sessile and pedunculate oaks, and there is a magnificent red oak near the site of Jack Wood House. But there are also beech trees, chestnuts, holly and blackthorn. Three main paths run through the woods and have been gradually widened by walkers. The Friends, together with RBG, are building deadhedging to protect the wildflowers and resurfacing paths so that walkers are not tempted to stray and do further damage.

But, even though many people are drawn here, the woods feel secretive. It feels as though the trees are watching you, waiting to see what you will do, or say. It feels as though they want to talk…

Access: Crown Woods Way SE18 3JA
Opening times: Crookston Road entrance always open
Facilities: Café and car park at Oxleas Woods,
Car park 8.00 am to 7.00 pm
Designation: SSSI, SINC of Metropolitan Importance
Size: 19.5 hectares (48 acres)

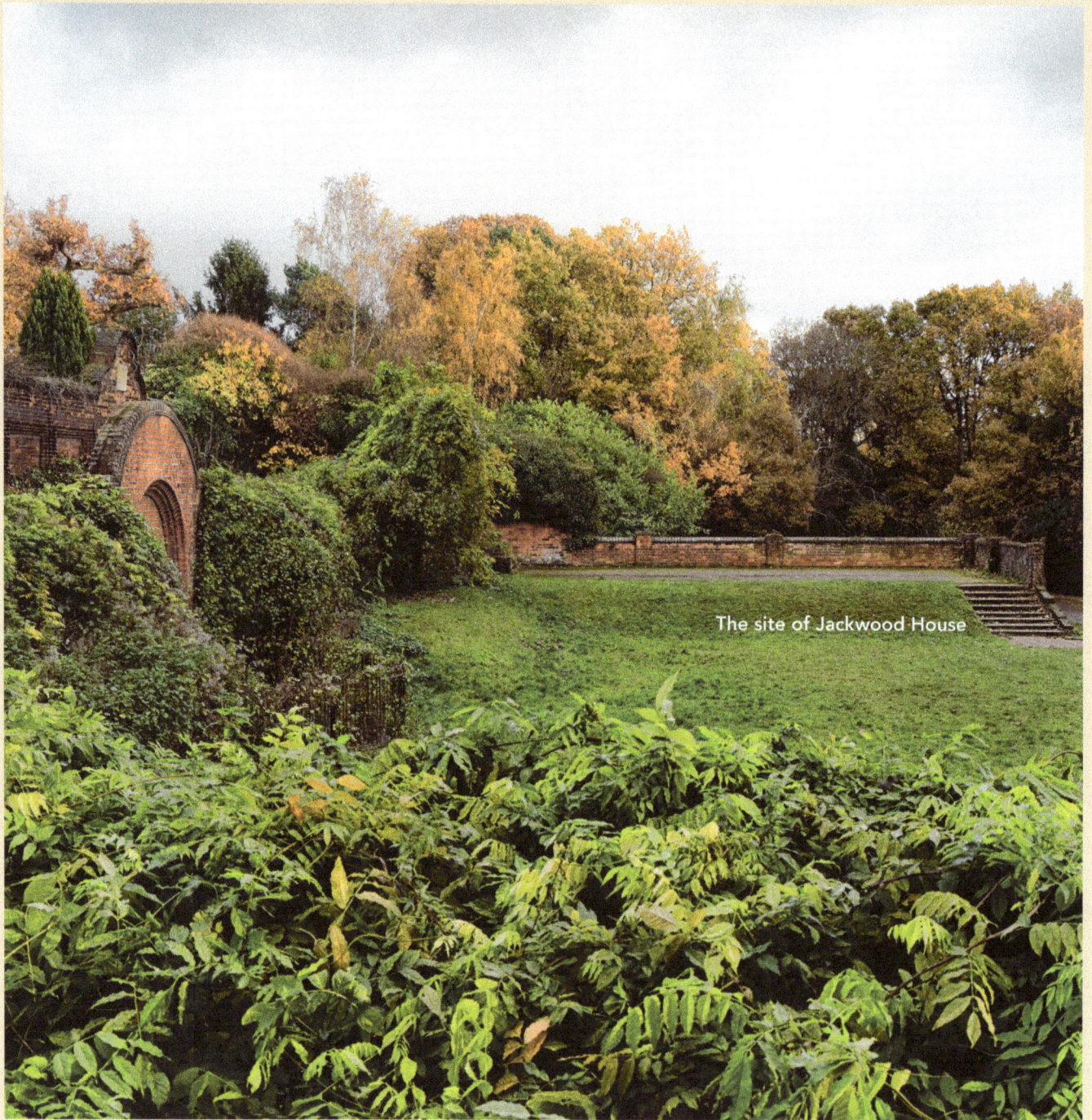

The site of Jackwood House

Jack Wood in the autumn

Oxleas Wood

In the late 1780s, Wood Lodge was built by a member of the Shaw family and stood on the site of today's café in Oxleas Wood. In 1809, Oxleas and Sheperdleas Woods were taken back by the Crown Estates, and in 1838, the Shaw family lost their lease of the Manor of Eltham.

Wood Lodge was damaged by a bomb in 1916, and the tenant left a few months later. The lodge was then handed to the War Department and used as an anti–aircraft unit. After the war it stood empty, became dilapidated and was finally pulled down in 1932. A café was built on the site in 1937, and today it is very popular and always busy!

There were two further large mansions in Oxleas Wood. Edward Wilde, the younger brother of Sir James Wilde of Jack Wood House, built Warren Wood c.1865. Later, it was the home of Col Bagnold, father to Enid Bagnold, the writer and author of *National Velvet*. It was finally demolished in the 1980s, and no trace remains.

Falconwood was built by Charles Wilde, 2nd Baron Truro, a cousin of Sir James Wilde, in c.1861. He leased forty acres of the wood and built a house where he lived till his death in 1891. From 1908, the lessee was the Baroness Catherine d'Erlanger and her husband. After WWI, they tried to convert the house into a hotel, but it was not successful, and by 1932, they had returned the lease to the Crown Commissioners. In the 1950s, the LCC bought the site and had demolished the mansion by the end of the decade. Only a grassy meadow remains today, with a path, once a curving drive off the Dover Road.

Summer Court stood to the east of Warren Wood but was demolished in the 1960s.

The LCC acquired the woods for public recreation in 1930, and they were opened to the public four years later. Ownership passed to the Borough of Greenwich in 1986.

Oxleas Meadow has an underground water reservoir which is controlled by Thames Water from a small building at the bottom of the meadow. The reservoir feeds the water tower on top of Shooters Hill.

Oxleas Wood is at least 8,000 years old and the largest area of Ancient Woodland close to the centre of London.

However, trees were still being harvested in the first half of the 1800s, and so trees on the southern side of the woods are likely to be secondary woodland.

This is the largest and most varied site on Shooters Hill, with thirty–two varieties of tree growing in the London clay. They are unique in having willow trees (grey willows and crack willows), Highclere holly, wild plums and aspens.

The dominant trees are pedunculate and sessile oak trees, but there are also birches, hazels and wild cherry trees. And there is the largest collection of wild service trees in London. Ashes and chestnuts were grown and harvested for hop poles in Kent, and coppicing in the past produced income. Coppicing has been re–introduced as a means of managing the woodlands.

The Friends of Oxleas Wood have a walking map which shows several ditches, dating perhaps from the mid–1800s, dug to improve drainage on the hill. The map also shows a stream which runs intermittently towards the east, and its damp edges encourage grasses such as carex pendula, carex sylvatica and yellow Pimpernel. Bluebells and wood anemones flower in remoter corners in the spring.

Coulthurst's Ride is a wide path running diagonally through the woods from the reservoir hut to Shooters Hill Road through an avenue of oak trees. It is named after William Coulthurst, a director of Coutts Bank who had shooting rights in the woods.

The woods can be very muddy in winter, but come and walk here in the spring and summer. The trees, especially the old oaks, are calming and you can wander for hours. And then linger in the very good café. Enjoy the view and just slow down...

Access: Crown Woods Lane SE18 3JA
Opening times: Always open
Facilities: Car park 8.00 am to 6.00 pm, café, toilets, benches, outdoor gym gear. The Green Chain Walk crosses the woods.
Designation: SSSI, Sinc of Metropolitan Importance
Size: c.58 hectares (143 acres)
Friends of Oxleas Wood: https://www.oxleaswoodlands.uk

ELTHAM

The dominant feature in Eltham's history is undoubtedly Eltham Palace.

'Eltham' is probably an Anglo–Saxon name meaning 'Elta's homestead'. The Domesday Book says Eltham was in the Hundred of Greenwich where it was held by Haimo the Sheriff from the Bishop of Liseux, who held the manor from Odo, the Bishop of Bayeux. When the sheriff died, the estates passed to the de Clare family, then the de Vesci family, and in 1296, to Antony Bek, the Bishop of Durham. He built a manor house and presented the manor to the Prince of Wales, later Edward II. The manor house became Eltham Palace.

In 1315, the Great Park and Middle Park were enclosed on either side of Eltham Palace. West Horne (later known as Horn Park) was added by further enclosures 150 years later. The parks were stocked with deer as these were hunting parks.

Eltham Palace was a favoured royal retreat away from the centre of London. It must have been very beautiful, as the palace and parks stood in heavily wooded countryside. Parliament met here in 1329 and 1375, tournaments were staged in the Tilt Yard, and the palace entertained important visitors from Europe. The decline started because Henry VIII preferred Greenwich and built a new palace there in the 16th century.

In the interregnum of 1649–60 many of the trees in the royal parks were cut down without permission, the deer were slaughtered and the palace fell into disrepair. The manor was sold but taken back by the Crown at the Restoration, and much of the land around the palace remains in Crown ownership in the 21st century.

Eltham village was on the main road between London and Maidstone; the Manor of Well Hall lay north of the village, and further to the north, the notorious Roman road of Watling Street led over Shooters Hill from London to Dover.

"The healthiness and pleasantness of its situation," says Hasted in 1797," makes it much resorted to by merchants and people of fortune for their summer residence, either in their houses or in handsome lodgings."[52]

Wealthy people who settled in Eltham built large homes such as Cliefden House (c.1720) with a large garden and a stable block at the back. The orangery (17th–18th century) belonged to Eltham House (demolished), and Eagle House (17th–18th century), which is now the Presbytery of Christ Church. Park Farm Place (18th century) to the north east of the village was a large country estate. Two pubs in the High Street date from the 18th century, the Greyhound and Rising Sun.

The expansion of the railways in the 19th century heralded change with stations opening at Mottingham (1866), New Eltham (1878), Well Hall (1895), and Shooters Hill (1908). Nevertheless, as late as 1912, Sir Walter Besant was able to

Below: Cliefden House

224

The Orangery

write, "Eltham village is, with its quaint inns and houses, a pleasant relic of the past."[53]

In 1900, Archibald Corbett bought land in Well Hall and Eltham Park and started building houses similar to his estates in Hither Green and Ilford. HM Office of Works built the remarkable Progress Estate in Well Hall in 1915. The Woolwich Council built the Page Estate in 1923, the Middle Park Estate in 1931–1936 and the Horn Park Estate from 1936 onwards. The Eltham Heights Estate was a private development north of Avery Hill Park in the 1930s, and the Coldharbour Estate was built after WWII.

The layout of most of these estates was influenced by the Garden City ideas first proposed by Sir Ebenezer Howard in 1898, but the council also understood the need for recreation grounds and parks and fortunately for residents incorporated these in their plans.

Mottingham lies south of Eltham and was recorded in the 9th century as Modingehema, probably meaning the land of Moda's people. It was an extraparochial hamlet owned by the prior and convent of St Andrew, Rochester, until the Dissolution of the Monasteries in the 16th century when it reverted to the Crown.

Before the railways arrived, Mottingham was sparsely populated: in the 1815 census only 131 people lived in a few houses and cottages along Mottingham Lane, and the few large mansions included Fairy Hall and Mottingham House.

New Eltham developed from the Pope Street hamlet south of Eltham and east of Mottingham in the 20th century, and here we find Southwood Park and Southwood Rough.

Essential reading:

Brooks, Roy, *The Story of Eltham Palace*, (1960, George Harrap & Co)
Gregory, R R C, *The Story of Royal Eltham*, (1909, republished by FamLoc)
Kennett, John, Articles on the history of Eltham in SENine Magazine
Spurgeon, Darrell, *Discover Eltham and its Environs*, (1992, Greenwich Guide-Books)
The Eltham Society, *Looking into Eltham*, 1980
Vincent, W T T, *Records of the Woolwich District, Vol II*, (1890, republished by FamLoc)

Avery Hill Park

In the 1970s Jerry Coleby–Williams worked at Avery Hill Nursery and Winter Garden. At that time "it remained the best example of a high Victorian garden estate in that part of London: a mansion with a sumptuous, glazed winter garden surrounded by an external winter garden and set in parkland planted with a huge range of choice plants and trees. Only while Crystal Palace was intact was Avery Hill outshone, and after the fire in 1936, Avery Hill became the most significant horticultural estate in South East London."[54]

Avery Hill Park had been a country estate since 1841, when James Boyd, a wealthy sugar refiner, built a mansion house in beautiful and ancient parkland. In 1888, Col J T North bought the old mansion from Anna–Maria Boyd.

John Thomas North (1842–96) was born in Leeds in Yorkshire where he was apprenticed as a mechanical engineer to Shaw, North and Watson. He then joined the John Fowler Steam Plough Works which exported to Chile and was sent there on contract in 1869 to maintain equipment. He started investing in nitrate production — sodium nitrate is used as a fertiliser and Chile has the world's largest deposits. By 1890, North and his associates controlled 70% of nitrate production in Chile. He diversified his business interests into coal, water and iron in Chile, the Congo and the UK, becoming one of the wealthiest men

in the UK and known as 'The Nitrate King'. Now he wanted social recognition, and in polite society, that required a mansion and garden.

He rebuilt Avery Hill Mansion into one of the grand country houses of the 19th century with a picture gallery, a Turkish bath and the best Winter Garden in London at the time, and now a Grade II listed building. The mansion and even the separate stable block had electric central heating! By 1891, his estate was over 272 hectares (672 acres) and stretched from Shooters Hill to New Eltham. Some of the estate was used for shooting and the remainder was farmland.

Outside, the Hon Mrs Evelyn Cecil remembers that in 1907 the formal terraced garden on the west side of the Winter Garden was "prettily planted with roses and fruit-trees," while tinkling sheep's bells in the meadows below added to the rural charm of the site.[55]

The Winter Garden was in three sections: the fernery with a pool and goldfish (on the east), and the drawing room conservatory and camellia house (on the west). Even in the 1970s, the central greenhouse had a Canary Island date palm and plants from South Africa, South America, Australia and California.

73

Meadows at Avery Hill

As an extension of the mansion, it was an awe–inspiring setting for grand social gatherings.

After Col North, died the estate was put up for auction. The LCC bought the mansion with twenty–eight acres of farmland in 1902, and it reopened in 1906 as Avery Hill Training College, the first training college for women teachers. Two years later, the college bought Southwood House. The college merged with Thames Polytechnic in 1985 and became part of the University of Greenwich. The mansion is now being converted to a boys' school in the Harris chain of schools.

Avery Hill Park remains open parkland with a variety of habitats including amenity and conservation grasslands, trees and woodland. The Friends list notable trees, of which two, a sweet chestnut and a pedunculate oak, are on the Ancient Tree Inventory. They have also surveyed the hedges, identifying some from the 17th century and earlier.

But today the formal terraced garden is sadly neglected and the Winter Garden is on the Buildings at Risk Register. The plants are depleted or missing, and the western fernery is empty. Despite the best efforts of two gardners, It is a heartbreaking sight and surely unnecessary? The future of this extraordinary glass building is sadly uncertain. It is rather like a ghost, watching and waiting, remembering the grand guests, the entertainments and rural idyll of the past, wondering what the future holds.

Access: Bexley Road SE9 2PG and park always open
Opening times: Winter Garden 10.00 am to 4.00 pm
Facilities: Café, toilets, sports grounds, children's play area, outdoor gym gear, outdoor table tennis tables. The Green Chain Walk and the Capital Ring run through the park.
Designation: Part SINC of Borough Importance Grade I, Green Flag Public Park,
Size: 32 hectares (79 acres)
Friends of Avery Hill Park: www.averyhillpark.org.uk

The central greenhouse

Above: The West Terrace overlooked by the Winter Garden
Below: The eastern fernery with Galatea Reclining on a Dolphin, by Leopoldo Ansiglioni, 1882

Pippenhall Meadows

The Meadows lie between the Pippenhall Allotments on Bexley Road and Butterfly Lane. A farmhouse stood here in the mid–17th century, and the Pippenhall Farm Dairy on Eltham High Street only closed in 1936. The land was part of Col North's estate before it was sold.

There are five meadows and some of the hedges date from c.1370. Is there ridge and furrow evidence in the south east corner? The centre is dry grasslands, and in the south of the site are springs, the source of the River Shuttle, which runs in ditches in the park and eventually joins the River Cray at Bexley.

The wildflower meadow, Henleys, is named after John de Henley who owned the manor of Henleys here in the late 13th century. The moated house stood in Conduit Field, below the conduit.

Horses graze on the meadows, and wildflowers are reappearing again and include narrow–leaved bird's foot trefoil, knapweed, erigeron and water dropwort. Only the field on Bexley Road, which sometimes has pyramid orchids, and the wildflower meadow are open. Butterfly Lane connects the meadows to the conduit.

Access: Bexley Road SE9 2PE
Designation: SINC of Metropolitan Importance
Size: c.6 hectares (c.15 acres)

The Conduit

Behind Holy Trinity Church on Southend Crescent is Little Conduit Field with the remains of a brick conduit head which probably dates from the 16th century.

The Eltham Warren Golf Club is situated across the road from Avery Hill Mansion. This was once a field in the countryside known as the Warren and used for grazing animals.

In the golf course grounds, alongside Gravel Pit Lane, there is a spring, and from here, wooden pipes made of elm, led water to the conduit head where it was somehow filtered, and then the water was piped to Eltham Palace. Water was also supplied to old houses in Court Yard.

Elm wood remains firm even when saturated with water, and this tells of a time when elm trees were plentiful in the area.

Access: Southend Crescent SE9 2SD
Opening times: Always open
Designation: Historic England Scheduled Monument Grade II, and Amenity Green Space
Size: 0.1 hectares (0.3 acres)

Coldharbour Estate

The land here was once woodland in the Great Park of Eltham Palace, but many of the trees were cut down in the interregnum and farms were established on the empty land when Sir John Shaw leased the Manor of Eltham in 1660

Chapel Farm and Coldharbour Farm stood here, with tenant farmers, but farming ended in 1947 when Woolwich Borough Council bought c.155 acres from the Crown Commissioners to build the Coldharbour Estate and the Coldharbour Leisure Centre. Queen Elizabeth, the King's grandmother, officially opened the estate in 1957.

Chapel Farmhouse (aka Townsend and Whitechapel Farm) stood approximately on the site of today's Coldharbour Leisure Centre. It was a cattle farm which sold its produce in the Chapel Farm Dairy on the High Street in Eltham. The open stream of the Little Quaggy provided water, and Chapel Farm Lane (now Court Road) connected the farm to the villages at Eltham and Mottingham.

Farming is hard work, but there was time for fun!

The farm had a football ground and hosted the Chapel Farm Cricket Club, first shown on a map of 1898. This became the Eltham Cricket Club where WG Grace played his final match on 25 July 1914. (He lived in Mottingham Lane from 1909 until his death in 1915.)

Coldharbour Farm lay to the south, with its farmhouse roughly at the junction of White Horse Hill and Elmstead Lane. It too was a dairy farm, which also produced oats and wheat, and kept pigs and horses as all farm machinery was horse drawn. This was one of the last working farms in London.

The Coldharbour Estate was for families made homeless during the Blitz of 1940–41 and mainly those living in Woolwich or Eltham. The ideals of the Garden City movement influenced the layout of the estate, with wide avenues such as Witherston Way and little greens amongst the houses such as Partridge Green, Buckler Gardens and Jason Walk. Homes have gardens and there are playing fields, parks, open meadows and allotments.

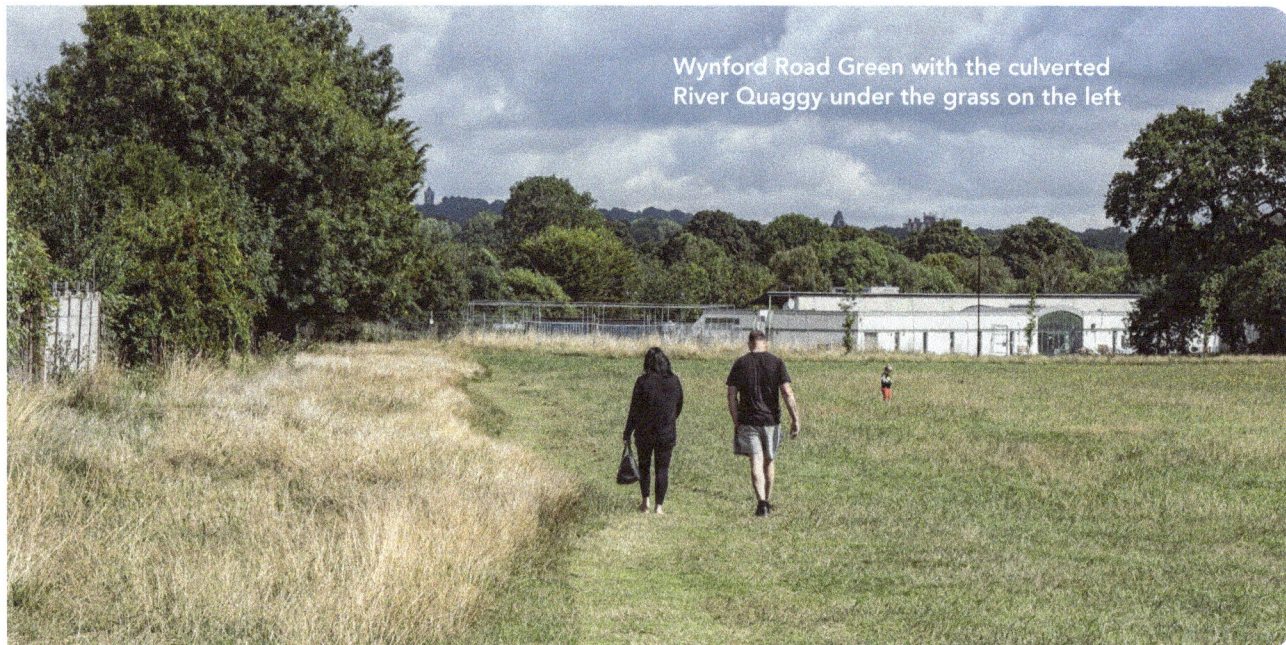

Wynford Road Green with the culverted River Quaggy under the grass on the left

Wynford Road Green

This open green field next to the Coldharbour Leisure Centre was listed as an athletic ground in 1934, with a pavilion on the line of the paved path crossing the field. The Little Quaggy is culverted on one side but imagine the meadow if the stream was open, attracting birds and insects, with flowers along its banks....

Altash Gardens

At the far end of the playing fields is the park of Altash Gardens, which includes a playground and outdoor gym. It is named after the mediaeval fields of Great and Little Altash in Mottingham.

There are elegant willow trees on this grassy and sloping site. A gap in the fence allows you into the 'Coldharbour Unleased Open Space', and here you can find magic. A wonderfully atmospheric meadow is filled with flowering grasses in June, and there is a particularly majestic willow tree, amongst other magnificent trees on the boundaries.

All sites can be accessed from
William Barefoot Drive SE9 3HU; they are always open and cover c.8 hectares (c.20 acres)

In spring 2023, 1500 whips were planted in the hope of creating three tiny forests.

Queen's Gardens

The small green opposite the dilapidated shopping centre on William Barefoot Drive, the main road through the estate, is Queen's Gardens. It offers a diagonal avenue of trees across the grass with a fenced-off dog-walking area.

The Course

On a breezy hillside, The Course offers two fields on the line of The Chase, an avenue of trees in Eltham Lodge which stands on the horizon. A children's playground, a ball court and a small hall divide the field, and at the southern end are fenced-off allotments. These two fields have a wonderful feel. The London plane trees, willows and new beech trees are elegant, and the pattern of mowing has allowed colourful grasses and wildflowers to develop.

The aspirations and ideas of the developers were high and admirable, and today's Friends and residents deserve support and attention to maintain those ideals.

Friends of Coldharbour Open Spaces: www.facebook.com

76b

Queen's Gardens

Altash Gardens children's playground

One of the newly planted tiny forests
in the fields next to Altash Gardens

Above: *The Friends of the Coldharbour Estate planting new trees just above the children's playground on The Course*

Below: *The Course, looking towards Eltham Lodge, now the club house of the Royal Blackheath Golf Club*

76d

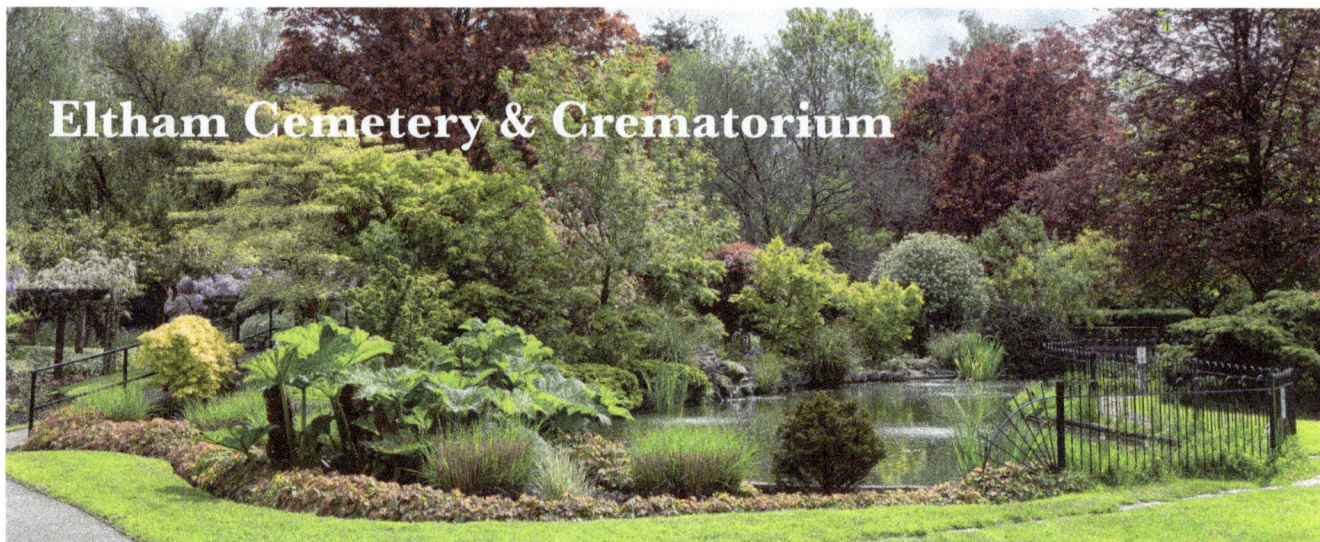

Eltham Cemetery & Crematorium

77

A narrow road from Crown Woods Way winds into the cemetery through a belt of oaks, beeches, chestnuts, sycamores, yews and maples to Riefield Road. The trees are perhaps the remains of Coalpits Wood which still appeared on the OS map of 1946 and was then overtaken by housing.

Coalpits Wood, Rennets Wood, and West Wood all belonged to the Lord of the Manor of Bexley, the Archbishop of Canterbury. Woods produced significant income for their owners: oak and hornbeam produced charcoal for domestic heating and cooking, for industrial processes, and for use in steam engines. The common term for charcoal was 'coal'; what we call coal today was known as 'seacoal' because it was imported into London by sea to replace wood. By the early 1800s, charcoal had mainly been replaced by coal.

In 1538, the manor passed to the Crown until James I gave it in 1614 to Sir John Spilman, the court goldsmith and jeweller, who shortly afterwards sold the manor to Sir William Camden, Clarenceaux King of Arms. Camden gifted the Manor of Bexley to the University of Oxford after his death in 1623 to endow the Camden Professorship of Ancient History, the oldest such position in England.

The cemetery was designed by Mr H W Tee, the Borough Engineer, and opened in 1935. There is a small wall of remembrance near the chapel and Kipling stones mark fifty-seven WWII graves. A curious statue marks the grave of an airman, LAC Ernest Francis Bennett, who was killed in a flying accident at Auchingilloch Hill Scotland on 28 December 1938, aged 23 years. Lt Cyril Gordon Martin was awarded the VC for action at Spanbroek Molen in 1915, and his ashes are buried at the crematorium. The ashes of Richmal Compton, the creator of the Just William stories, are scattered in the garden.

Eltham Crematorium and its Chapel of Remembrance, a small replica of Liverpool's Cathedral, opened in 1956. The Crematorium is peaceful, set in a softer landscape with curving paths, shrub borders and an informal rockery with a pond. At the far east of the site is a woodland area on undulating ground with interesting trees and curving paths. The site was awarded a Gold Medal in London in Bloom 2024.

Access: Crown Woods Way SE9 2RF
Opening times: 9.00 am to dusk but check website
Facilities: Toilets, shop, car park
Designation: Cemetery
Size: 10.6 hectares (26 acres)
https://www.royalgreenwich.gov.uk

Eltham Green

Eltham Green escapes attention today, and is perhaps unremarkable, but it was once very different.

Houses nos.1–13 Eltham Green Road were built c.1840, and they were quite isolated, surrounded by farmland and overlooking the common land of Eltham Green on the main road between Lee and Eltham.

In 1878, Robert Butts tells us, the road was lined with old elms but by this time Eltham Green was "but the ghost of its former self, when on May–Day and rustic holidays it witnessed the mirth, and was vocal with the unrestrained delight to those to whom rest from labour is delight."[56] The pound remained on the corner of Green Way and Eltham Hill and today it is still a patch of green.

Now, Eltham Green is in different sections: the expanse of grass between Eltham Hill and Green Way, the land in the roundabout, the small meadow alongside Eltham Green Road and the developing wildflower meadow alongside the new Kidbrooke Village Estate. Here, Robert Butts asks us to "rest awhile on the bridge under which a clear stream (the Quaggy) flows with a gentle ripple … coming from, and passing on through rich water-meadows."[57] The traffic whizzes past, but I am sure Butts would be pleased with the wildflower meadow and the little stream in neighbouring Sutcliffe Park.

The McDonald's on the edge of the roundabout was once the Yorkshire Grey pub, built c.1930s, around the same time as the Middle Park Estate and known for unlicensed boxing, particularly a gruelling bout between Lenny 'The Guv'nor' McLean and Brian 'Mad Gypsy' Bradshaw![58]

Access: Eltham Green SE9 5J
Opening times: Always open
Facilities: None
Designation: Public Open Land, Amenity Green Space
Size: 2 hectares (5 acres)

Eltham Palace

Christmas Lights Festival

Eltham Palace is a stunning site in South East London!

A royal palace was established here when Antony Bek, the Bishop of Durham, presented his moated manor house to the Prince of Wales who became Edward II in 1307.

Future kings developed the site: the stone bridge over the north moat was built by Richard II in 1396, and in the 1470s, Edward IV built the great hall with its imposing chestnut hammerbeam roof. Eltham Palace was the favoured royal palace until the 16th century when Henry VIII built Greenwich Palace.

In 1649, at the start of the interregnum, Parliament ordered a survey of the Manor of Eltham. The palace was found to be in disrepair, and the chapel and the great hall were the only furnished rooms. The three parks of the Great Park, Middle Park and Horn Park (aka Lee Park) covered c.1,214 acres and had c.7,700 trees. About 4,000 were old, and the rest were suitable for shipbuilding. The deer had been destroyed, but the Act for the sale of Crown Lands, 1649, gave official approval for the cutting of timber for the growing navy.

John Evelyn's criticism in 1656 of Nathaniel Rich, that he destroyed the woods and park, is probably incorrect; Col Rich and soldiers had been sent to stop the poaching.

The layout of Eltham Palace, the surrounding fields and the Great Park (now the Blackheath Golf Club) has hardly changed since the 17th and 18th centuries and much of the land around the palace remained in Crown ownership well into the 20th century.

In the 1930s, Stephen and Virginia Courtauld took a ninety–nine–year lease from the Crown and started the first serious renovation, commissioning Seely and Paget to build an art–deco mansion which incorporated the great hall. The Courtaulds only stayed until 1944, when the Army Educational Corps took over. In 1995, English Heritage assumed management of the site and completed another major restoration programme four years later. The building and gardens are Grade II*.

The gardens have been restored to the 1930s design. There is a Japanese rockery on the east side, and on the west side of the palace is a sunken rose garden and pond with two further garden rooms. The south moat wall has a long

The 14th century stone bridge
on the north side of Eltham Palace

The Japanese Garden and the moat in June

herbaceous border which was re–planted in 2000 by Isabelle van Groeningen. It is the north side under the stone bridge, less frequented, which is most atmospheric, and where you can feel the age of the site.

The moat bank and parkland to the south and east are managed as meadow, i.e. hay is taken in July and it is then mown up to Christmas. This has encouraged wildflowers such as oxlips, primroses, wood anemone, bluebells and snakeshead fritillaries.

The Courtaulds planted some wonderful trees which have now matured: an Indian bean tree, tulip tree, walnut and bay trees. And there are majestic oaks and London plane trees.

There are still open fields to the south of Eltham Palace — King John's Field and Middle Park Field. They are not accessible to the public but create a magical illusion of countryside. And the illusion continues to the west of the palace in the fields on the far side of King John's Walk.

Today the site is an elegant park, beautifully maintained, and an important historical heritage. Mainly quiet and peaceful, it attracts visitors at all times of the day, in all seasons, and the Christmas Lights Festival or other Christmas entertainments are fun!

Access: Court Lane SE9 5AG
Opening times: Please see website
Facilities: Car park, café, children's play area, toilets
Designation: Fields SINCs of Local Importance Grade I
Size: 35 hectares including the fields (86 acres)
Eltham Palace: www.english-heritage.org.uk

The rose garden

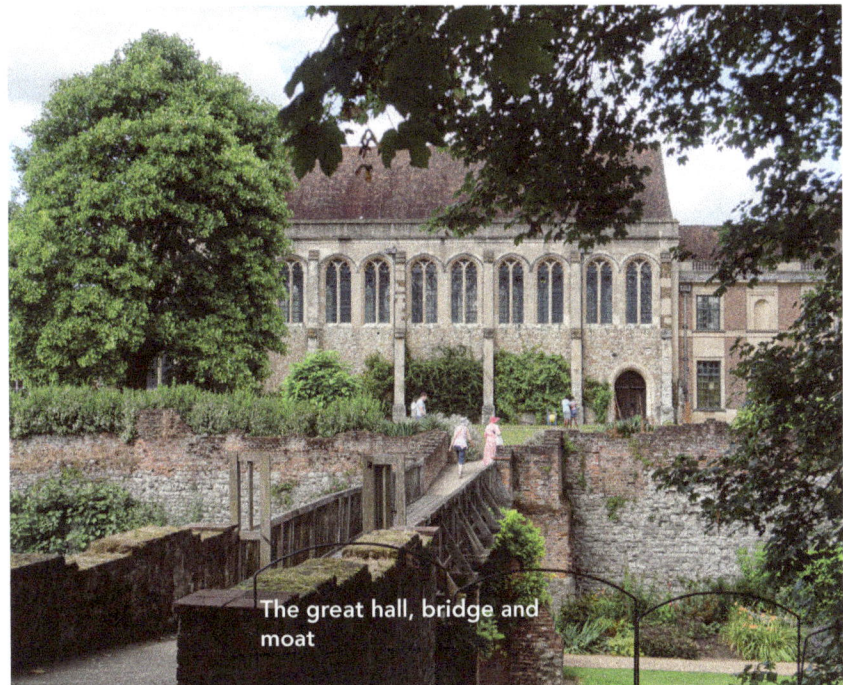
The great hall, bridge and moat

Eltham Park South

Eltham Park South is open and pleasant, with views to Shooters Hill. The grassland is mown sports fields with an avenue of mature trees on the Capital Ring Path alongside Eltham Warren Golf Club, and for a few short weeks in spring, the cherry trees on Glenesk Road are glorious!

Park Farm Place (later Eltham Park House) stood in the countryside to the north east of Eltham village. Sir William James bought the estate and farm in c.1775 and rebuilt the house, enclosing its surrounding land to create a park. Lady James built Severndroog Castle in his memory on estate land at Shooters Hill. In 1829, when the estate was auctioned, it covered 143 acres and stretched from Shooters Hill down to today's Bexley Road.

In 1810, the name of the property was changed to Eltham Park. Archibald Corbett bought the estate and more land in 1899 from Thomas Jackson, paying £50,000 for 334 acres which included the mansion and farm buildings. The Bexleyheath railway line had opened in 1895, and Corbett anticipated a demand for new houses for commuters travelling into London and the City for work.

The layout of Corbett's Eltham Estate is similar to his housing development in Hither Green, Lewisham; it is laid out in a grid with churches but no pubs, as he disapproved of alcohol. The demand for new houses stopped with the outbreak of WWI, so Corbett sold forty–one acres to the local council and this became Eltham Park South.

Eltham Park was planned as sports fields, including tennis courts and a putting green, but while Woolwich Council and the LCC argued over costs, the land was used for grazing sheep! Eltham Park Lido opened in 1924, and it was used by the Eltham Training and Swimming Club which undertook long-distance swims, including cross–channel events. This was the club which trained Tom Gregory, who swam the Channel when he was eleven years old. The lido closed in 1988.

Today the park is family–oriented, a place to relax outside, enjoy refreshments from the café and meet friends. And every year PARKSfest, organised by the Greenwich Parks Forum, offers a day of music and fun.

The A2 and the railway line divide Eltham Park South and Eltham Park North, which are connected via a footbridge over the traffic.

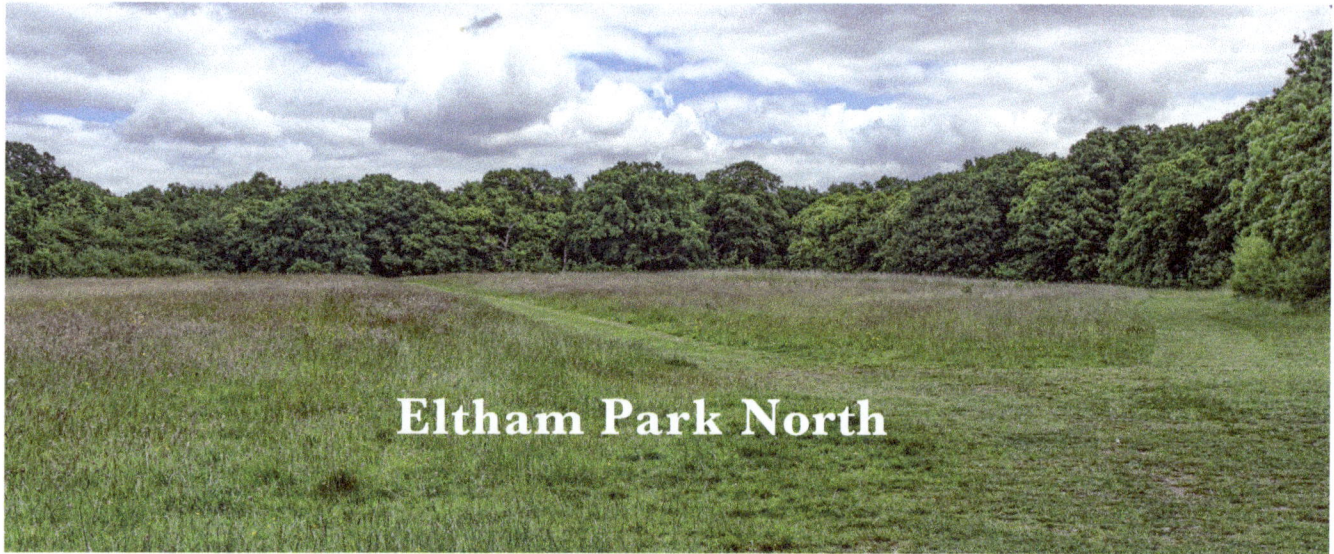

Eltham Park North

Eltham Park North is more secretive.

Archibald Corbett donated land for Eltham Park North to the LCC in 1926, and Sheperdleas Wood was added to the park in 1936. The park lies between the Rochester Way in the north and the A2 and railway line in the south.

The entrance from Eltham Park Gardens is up steeply sloping open grassland. On the left are views towards Lewisham and the ridge, which was once the Great North Wood, the centre of London and the Isle of Dogs.

On top of the hill you will find the Long Pond, which was probably excavated between 1800 and 1830, and was a private boating lake in the mid–19th century. (The OS map of 1862–73 shows a boat house at the southern tip of the lake.) The lake supports common water birds and is overhung with old, twisted willow trees.

Beyond the pond is a meadow with false oatgrass, perennial ryegrass and crested dog's–tail. And in the spring and summer, common knapweed, oxeye daisies, clovers, cowslips, buttercups and other wildflowers add a delightful profusion of pinks, whites and yellows. This area is a SINC of Borough Importance Grade II.

But the real joy is the woods surrounding the meadow to the north and east. Sheperdleas Woods are Ancient Woodland, which means they have been undisturbed by farming for at least 400 years. They are actually part of Oxleas Woods, from which they were cut off by the Rochester Way.

The trees are mainly oak, but there is also hawthorn, hazel, birch, ash, wild cherry and the wild service tree which is an indicator of Ancient Woodland. And there are swathes of bluebells in the spring! The park is relatively unfrequented, and so the paths are narrow and the bluebells and wood anemones can thrive and spread. Long may they last!

Access: Eltham Park South from Glenesk Road SE9 1AN, Eltham Park North from Eltham Park Gardens SE9 1QW
Opening times: Always open
Facilities at Eltham Park South: children's playground, tennis courts, table tennis tables, outdoor gym gear, football and cricket pitches, café, toilets, free car park. The Green Chain Walk and Capital Ring Path run through both parks
Designation: Green Flag Public Parks, Sheperdleas Woods SSSI, SINC of Borough Importance Grade II
Size: Eltham Park South 16.8 hectares (41 acres), Eltham Park North 8.6 hectares (21 acres)

Fairoak Drive

The Eltham Heights Estate was built by J E Webb and Co on land which was released by the Crown Estate for development. It was originally Coalpits Wood and Avery Hill farm, and the farmhouse stood at the junction of today's Bexley Road and Crown Woods Road.

By 1938, the three main roads of Riefield Road, Crown Woods Road and Coalpits Wood Road had been laid down, and houses were promoted for sale at the same time. The developer aimed to incorporate "the natural beauty of the Landscape with the charm of inspired Architecture. Part of the Estate is beautifully wooded and the trees are being carefully preserved; where a plot has no existing trees in the front garden, ornamental trees will be planted behind the forecourt walls."[59]

The green space of Fairoak Drive is a triangular green in the middle of housing, and on the OS map published in 1934, it seems to be the triangular space in Coalpits Wood, defined by footpaths through the woods.

Fairoak Drive Green is a small reminder of the woods which once covered Eltham. There are beautiful and mature trees on the green that predate the housing — pines, oaks and a wonderful hornbeam tree — as well as some young birch trees, but sadly the atmosphere of woodlands has gone. We should at least be grateful for the green.

Access: Fairoak Drive SE9 2QG
Opening times: Always open
Facilities: None
Designation: Amenity Green Space
Size: 0.6 hectares (1.5 acres)

81

Fairy Hill Park

82

Fairy Hill Park was once part of Sir John Shaw's estate on Eltham Palace grounds.

Today, the park is a very attractive recreation ground with good facilities for children and adults. The small woodland areas on the western and southern boundaries are pleasing, populated with horse chestnut, oak, hazel and birch trees and an undergrowth of bramble and ivy. The woodland path can be very muddy and would benefit, perhaps, from a wood chip covering.

The Little Quaggy skirts the western edge of the park, but it is enclosed in a culvert underground and only reappears in the south east corner of The Tarn. The Green Chain Walk crosses the park.

The park opened in 1938 and is named after Fairy Hall in Mottingham, which was a country villa owned by Henry Bathurst, a barrister and judge in the court of common pleas. He was also the 1st Baron Apsley and the 2nd Earl Bathurst. Apsley House was his London home, and Fairy Hall was one of his country retreats. By 1857, the owner was James Hartley, a shipowner, who rebuilt the mansion.

In 1889, the Royal Navy bought Fairy Hall because the original Royal Navy School in New Cross (today's Goldsmiths, University of London) had become too small. Since 1976, the building has been an independent educational institution, Eltham College.

There is a curious old oak tree near the tennis courts; could this once have been part of The Chase, an avenue leading from Eltham Lodge to today's park of The Course?

The park is well cared for and very pleasant.

Access: Crossmead SE9 3AA, Broad Lawn SE9 3XD
Opening times: 8.00 am to dusk
Facilities: Tennis courts, basketball court, cycle track, outdoor gym gear, children's playground, seats
Designation: Green Flag Public Park
Size: 4.7 hectares (11.5 acres)
Friends of Fairy Hill Park: www.facebook.com

Falconwood Field

Falconwood Field was one of the fields in this area in the late 1800s. Was this where kings had flown their falcons centuries before?

Until the end of the 19th century the field was bordered by West Wood to the east, which was in the Manor of Bexley and owned by the University of Oxford. Woodland was cleared in 1895, and replaced with Westwood Farm, and by 1914, the whole of the Westwood had been cut down for residential development. In the 1930s, New Ideal Homesteads bought the farm and built Falconwood Park, a housing estate, which is in the borough of Bexley

The 2nd Lord Truro, Charles Robert Wilde, built Falconhurst in 1864–67 on Crown land at Shooters Hill, and it became known as Falconwood. Falconwood Field, down the hill and below Oxleas Wood, remembers the lost mansion in its name, or was the mansion named after the field? Falconwood Field was acquired by RBG in 1936.

83

The Falconwood Model Railway was set up in 1975 in the north east corner of the field by the Welling and District Model Engineering Railway Society. In 2022, the club relocated to Hall Place because National Grid is building a tunnel head house in the field to meet an increased demand for power in London.

A small patch of Ancient Woodland still exists at the north east corner of the field and was once part of Oxleas Wood before being cut off by the Rochester Way and Welling Road.

Come here in the summer when the field is ablaze with wildflowers and flowering grasses – it is lovely!

Access: Rochester Way SE9 2RE or Welling Way DA16 2RP
Opening times: Always open
Facilities: None
Designation: Amenity Green Space
Size: 6.4 hectares (16 acres)

Gravel Pit Lane

Gravel Pit Lane in Eltham is a centuries–old green lane which has miraculously escaped the developers.

The lane is marked on a map of 1801 by William Mudge when it led through farmland and woods passing Falconwood to Welling. Now offers a magical little walk alongside the Warren Golf Course, and between two busy main roads, Bexley Road and Riefield Road.

The very substantial oak trees in the lane point to the age of the path, and two are listed in the Ancient Tree Inventory. Ancient hedges, of field maple, holly, hazel and crab apple, line the lane which is crossed by a stream from the golf course. Is this the stream which leads to The Conduit?

84

The golf course started in 1890 when a group of friends played on a field here. They decided to form a club and rented seventeen acres of a field known as Warren Field. By 1910 the nine–hole course had reached its current size.

I love walking in this lane. I love the timeless feeling. I love the peace of the trees.

Access: Bexley Road SE9 2PE and Riefield Road SE9 2RA
Opening times: Always open
Facilities: None
Designation: SINC of Borough Importance Grade I, Public Footpath, on Green Chain Walk
Length: 0.8 kms (0.5 miles)

Horn Park

Sports fields on top of the hill

85

West Horne, of 345 acres, was enclosed in 1465 as one of the three parks of the Eltham Palace estate. A survey of 1605 found 240 deer and 2,740 oak trees, of which the mature trees were valuable for shipbuilding in Deptford.

Sadly, the parkland was denuded and the deer destroyed before or during the interregnum, and when Nathaniel Rich bought the palace estates in 1648, West Horne was converted into farmland.

By the 19th century, Horn Park Farm, of 221 acres arable land and pastures, stood here and was owned by the Crown. William Morris was the tenant farmer. Morris also farmed Lee Green Farm. When his lease expired in 1860, Thomas Blenkiron (1829–1894) leased the farm. He was a silk merchant but his father, William Blenkiron (1807–71), used the land to graze his racehorses. (See Queenscroft Park.)

The Wood family were the last farmers at Horn Park Farm, and when their lease expired in 1930, the Woolwich Council cleared their orchards and market gardens for new housing. The Horn Park Estate was completed after WWII, served by the Dutch House pub and a new school.

Today, the park is mostly grassland with a hedge separating the sports fields from the meadows below. Developing secondary woodland covers the top of the hill, where a delightful path, spread with wood chippings, hides in the trees. The Friends have been planting trees in the little woodland since 2008.

In the sloping meadow, there are mature and beautiful willow trees, and here the Friends are creating a new coppice with whips and trees donated by Greenwich Mutual Aid, the Woodland Trust and the Conservation Volunteers. They include native species which will tolerate exposed sites and include hazel, downy birch, hawthorn, goat willow and crab apple. And one thousand daffodils are planted every year.

One day, the hillside down to the valley of the Quaggy will have returned to the peace of the trees, thanks to the vision and hard work of the Friends. This quiet park offers an enjoyable and very attractive walk at the end of a day, and is relatively unknown.

Access: Alnwick Road SE12 9EZ, Gavestone Crescent SE12 9BT
Opening times: 6.00 am to 8.00 pm
Facilities: Outdoor gym gear, skateboard park, children's playground, sports field, multipurpose ball court, seats
Designation: Green Flag Public Park
Size: 6.7 hectares (16.5 acres)
Friends of Horn Park: www.facebook.com

Above: *The park in Spring*
Below: *Meadows in summer, looking towards Eltham Palace on the opposite rise*

King John's Walk

An old countryside right of way once connected Eltham to Mottingham, passing the palace and crossing fields and streams, and today this is King John's Walk. Who was it named after? There are several 'Johns' associated with Eltham Palace but only two who were royal.

Prince John of Eltham was born at the palace on 15 August 1316, the second child and youngest son of Edward II of England and Isabella of France. Edward II had given Eltham to his queen, as a gift, and she often stayed there. Prince John was a strong supporter of his elder brother, who became Edward III and was apparently a ruthless military commander. However, he died when only twenty years old in 1336 and is buried in Westminster Abbey.

King John of France (1319–64), Jean le Bon, was defeated and captured by the English at the Battle of Poitiers in 1356, taken to England and held to ransom. In 1360, he was released to return to France in exchange for hostages which included his son Louis, and when Louis escaped in 1364, King John voluntarily returned to England.

According to Jean Froissart: "After spending two days at Canterbury, he rode on towards London and, travelling in short stages, came to Eltham where the King and Queen of England were waiting to receive him with a great company of knights and ladies. He arrived on a Sunday in the afternoon, and between then and supper there was time for much dancing and merriment. It would be impossible for me to record all the honours with which the King and Queen of England received King John, but finally he left Eltham and entered London."[60] The King died in London the same year.

Of the two, is Jean le Bon, King John, perhaps the most likely candidate?

Today this old path hides away below the palace, on top of the hill, leading downwards past fields with donkeys and horses, across the Sidcup bypass, and past the Mottingham Farm lands (now riding stables) to Mottingham Lane, which was once the heart of old Mottingham Village. The view is over the Middle Park and Horn Park Estates, then towards Blackheath, and Canary Wharf and the Shard are on the western horizon. The path is paved and a pleasant and breezy walk at all times of the year.

Access: Middle Park Avenue SE9 5RP or Court Yard SE9 5QE
Opening times: Always open
Facilities: None
Designation: Public Right of Way, Green Chain Walk
Length: c.1.5 kms (c.1 mile)

86

Opposite: Looking across Vista Field to Canary Wharf and the City
Below: King John's Walk in December

Above: The donkeys,which gave rides to children on Blackheath, enjoying retirement in the field next to King John's Walk

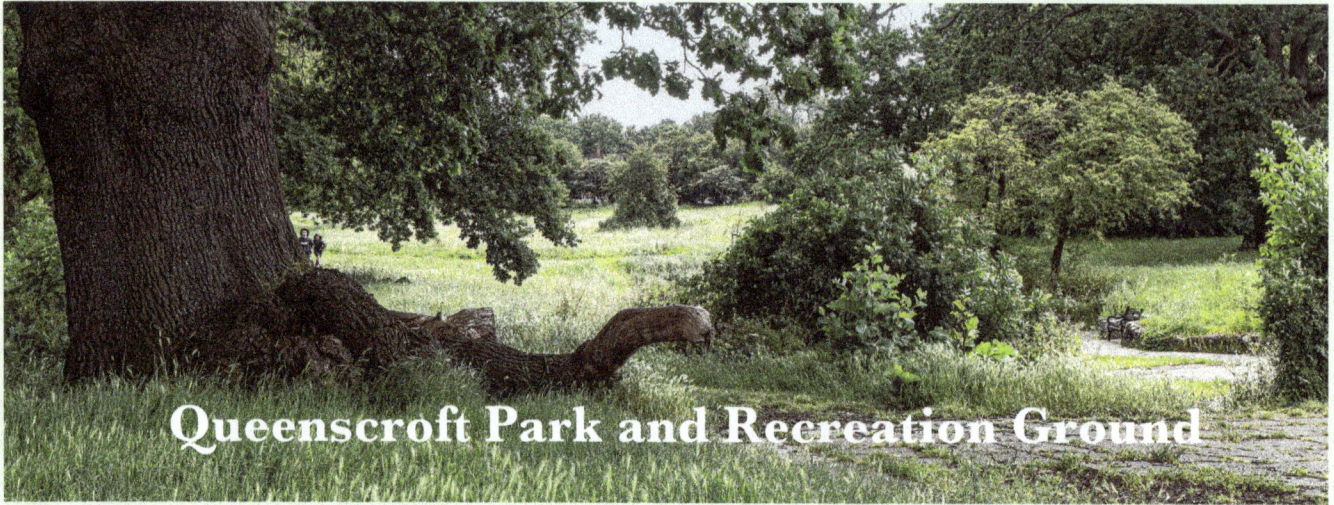

Queenscroft Park and Recreation Ground

87

Queenscroft Park was once in the Middle Park of Eltham Palace. The parliamentary survey of 1649 found the park covered 333 acres, with a lodge, but the deer had been killed. There were 324 trees in addition to the 1,000 trees identified as suitable for shipbuilding. After the Restoration, Sir John Shaw leased the Eltham Palace Estates, and Middle Park was farmed to produce food for Eltham Lodge.

The site became noteworthy again with William Blenkiron, a wealthy manufacturer whose passion was breeding racehorses. He established an extremely successful stud at Horn Park Farm and then bought Middle Park in 1852. In 1866, he founded the Middle Park Stakes, a race for two–year olds which is still run at Newmarket. During his life, this was the most successful stud in England, producing four Derby winners and with establishments at Middle Park, Esher and Waltham Cross. After his death, his son sold the stud in accord with his father's will, and the land reverted to farmland.

The park is named after Queenscroft, a redbrick house c.1720 at 150 Eltham Hill, and a Grade II listed building.

By 1914, Oakhurst Farm lay to the north of the park, but in 1927, Eltham Hill School was built on the farmland. The new Middle Park housing estate followed in 1931–36. By 1952, the farm had disappeared, replaced by Queenscroft Park with a model boating lake and paddling pool.

I close my eyes and imagine a beautiful park rich in biodiversity. The small stream is restored and gurgles down the palace hillside to the long pond, surrounded by rushes and yellow flag irises which hosts an array of birds, even a heron! Children investigate pond life here and learn about nature. And alongside this is the circular pool where children can frolic in summer, as in Hornfair Park. Mature oak and lime trees stand on the school boundary, and there are copses of young trees. On the steep hillsides, the grasses and wildflowers are luxuriant in spring and early summer, and the sights and sounds refresh the spirit.

I linger in this beautiful vision and then I open my eyes and find there is a very nice new playground for children, but the ponds are grassed over and new trees are struggling.

It is a sad sight, but a huge opportunity for the new Friends of the park. Here is a chance to create one of the most beautiful parklands in the borough and one which is rich in biodiversity. The Friends deserve everyone's support and encouragement.

Access: Queenscroft Road SE9 5EJ
Opening times: ALways open
Facilities: Children's playground outdoor gym gear, seats
Designation: Public Park
Size: 5.2 hectares (12.8 acres)
Friends of Queenscroft Park: www.facebook.com

The lost pond in Queenscroft Park

Royal Blackheath Golf Club

88

John Shaw (1615–1680) was a wealthy banker with business in London and Antwerp. He supported Prince Charles financially while he was in exile and allowed him a secure line of communication to the Royalist cause in England. At the restoration of the monarchy he was rewarded with a knighthood, then a baronetcy and several offices of state, including Trustee of the Queen's lands. More significantly, Shaw and two colleagues took over the equivalent of HMRC, i.e. all incoming tax into London!

In 1663, Sir John was granted a lease of the Manor of Eltham, which stayed in the family until 1838, when it reverted to the Crown. Sir John was buried in the family vault below the Church of St John the Baptist in Eltham.

Eltham Palace had gradually fallen into disrepair, so Sir John used the palace buildings as farm buildings and built a new house for himself. Eltham Lodge was designed by Hugh May and built in 1663–64 on the site of the keeper's lodge in the Great Park. According to Pevsner it is "an outstanding example of early Restoration domestic design"[61] and a Grade I listed building.

The estates were vast. In addition to the palace and its fields, there were the enclosed Great Park, Middle Park and Horn Parks, a total of c.1,650 acres, as well as manorial rights in the parish of Eltham, Mottingham, Woolwich and part of Foots Cray.

Hugh May also laid out the grounds around Eltham Lodge with terraces, parterres near the house, woodland gardens further down the hill with pools and rides, and a walled kitchen garden and orchard to the east. On 14 July 1664, John Evelyn speaks of "the orangery and aviary handsome, and a very large plantation about it."[62]

Eltham Lodge had various owners after the Shaw family, but in 1892, the Crown Estate granted a lease to the Eltham Golf Club, which merged with the Royal Blackheath Golf Club in 1923. Today, Eltham Lodge is the clubhouse of the Royal Blackheath Golf Club.

Do visit on an Open Day and do read John Bunney's book, *Eltham Lodge: Where Perfection meets Convenience*.

Access: Not open to the public
Designation: Part SINC of Metropolitan Importance, SINC Grade 2 in south of the site; part SSSI; Private Golf Club
Size: 44 hectares (110 acres)
RBGC: https://www.royalblackheath.com

The Club House, formerly Eltham Lodge

The
Tarn

The Tarn is a beautiful small park around a lake and alongside the Royal Blackheath Golf Club.

Sir John Shaw of Eltham Lodge succeded as 4th baronet in 1738, and in the mid–18th century he set about renovating the house and developing the estate. The pond was enlarged to create a pleasure and boating lake, today's substantial and irregularly shaped Tarn. In 1839, the lake was called Starbucks Pond, named after a local family. 'Starbucks' remains a local name: in the 20th century, Harry Starbuck ran the Abbey Arms pub and the Harrow pub. He was also known for bare–knuckle fighting! And the name continues in Starbuck Close on the east of the park.

An ice well of c.1760 which serviced Eltham Lodge stands near the lake where ice would be cut in winter. It is a Grade II listed building, built of brick with a domed roof, and the ice was stored underground. (Manor House Gardens in Lewisham has a similar but more elaborate icehouse which is sometimes open to the public.)

In 1934, Woolwich Council bought land, including woodland and the lake, from the Royal Blackheath Golf Course to create a public park. The wooded north east corner is a bird sanctuary which is closed to the public and covers almost half the site.

The lake with its small island is a haven for birds, and the Friends' website lists the many species which can be seen here, in addition to the foxes and bats. The lake is fed by the Little Quaggy, which enters The Tarn in a concrete channel in the south east corner of the lake. There is also a drain from the golf course, which feeds into the lake. Would

The Tarn perhaps benefit from filtration beds here, such as those in Gallions Lake? The outflow is through a grill near Court Road, and the river is enclosed until it reappears in the grounds of the Mottingham Farm Riding Centre and joins the Quaggy near the Dutch House pub.

The Friends of The Tarn are essential to this park! They were set up in 2008 and are there every week, digging, weeding, planting and repairing, and their care and commitment are very clear as you walk down the slope from the road into a haven of calm. Their wildflower meadow attracts butterflies, the spring bulbs are abundant and beautiful, and they have installed nesting boxes and bee homes to help local school children with nature study lessons. Around the water you can find lesser reedmace, reed grass and the poisonous hemlock water dropwort.

The Tarn is below the level of Court Road, and its situation and the many trees create a quiet and sheltered site. This is a park which feels loved, and it envelops you with caring as you walk round, or just sit and enjoy it in quiet company with other visitors.

Access: Court Road SE9 5AQ
Opening times: 8.00 am to dusk
Facilities: Picnic area, benches, storage room and toilets, on the Green Chain Walk
Designation: Green Flag Public Park, SINC of Local Importance, Outstanding Achievement Award London in Bloom 2024
Size: 3.6 hectares (8.9 acres)
Friends of The Tarn: www.thetarn.org

89

St John the Baptist Churchyard

The Church of St John the Baptist looks austere, standing at the corner of two busy main roads and closed off by a wall. But walk into the churchyard stretching out along Well Hall Road and you will find the 'rural flavour' in which Isabella Holmes delighted.[63]

Purple knapweed, yellow greater celandine, oxeye daisies, meadow buttercups, feverfew and grasses such as oatgrass and vernal grass have been reported. The gravestones tilt into the grass on the rough and uneven ground, and many are covered with moss and lichen. Large old yew trees lour at us from the edges of the churchyard, dark and poisonous, while mature sycamore, lime and oak trees shield the churchyard from Well Hall Road and a stately Cedar of Lebanon guards one corner.

The Domesday Book did not generally record churches, but there is a record of the Manor of Eltham, and so it is likely that there has been a church on the site for nearly 1,000 years. The church was rebuilt in the late 17th century at the expense of Sir John Shaw, and again in 1871–75 by the architect Sir Arthur W Blomfield whose building is Grade II listed today. The vicarage stood next to the church and had extensive gardens which were taken over when the churchyard was extended, probably in the 20th century. This section hides away beyond a gateway on the west side of the graveyard.

There are many interesting graves and memorials in the churchyard, but just take care as you walk round because the ground is very uneven.

Yemmerrawanyea Kebbarah, a young aborigine of the Eora nation, was brought to England with Woollarawarra Bennelong in 1793 by Arthur Philip, the first Governor of New South Wales. Sadly, the young man soon fell ill and was moved to Eltham to be in cleaner country air, but he died a year later. His memorial stone is embedded in the churchyard wall on Well Hall Road.

A plaque to Thomas Doggett, who in 1715 founded an annual race on the Thames, the Doggett's Coat and Badge,

is on the outer south wall of the church; Col J T North of Avery Hill has a red granite memorial; and Sir William James of Eltham Park Place is buried under a large chest tomb but also remembered in Severndroog Castle; and William Blenkiron has an obelisk memorial.

The dead of both World Wars are commemorated on twenty–one Kipling stones placed by the Commonwealth War Graves Commission, but most are invisible, buried under brambles and long grass. And a small memorial stone on the churchyard wall commemorates men who died in the South African war of 1899–1902.

This churchyard is unexpectedly beautiful and peaceful.

Access: Eltham High Street SE9 1DH
Opening times: The churchyard is always open
Facilities: Benches
Designation: Churchyard, SINC of Local Importance
Size: 1.6 hectares (4 acres)
www.elthamchurch.org.uk

Gateway into the 20th century churchyard

90

St John the Baptist Churchyard in June

Sidcup Road Grassland & Harmony Wood

If you live in South East London, you have probably been up and down the Sidcup bypass many times, concentrating hard on keeping to the speed limit and avoiding impatient drivers.

But hidden between the road and the railway line is a little piece of paradise. Yes, you can hear the traffic, if you want to hear it, but if you concentrate on the trees, the meadows, wildflowers and the views, even the cars will disappear. Sidcup Road Grassland and Harmony Wood are also known as the Great Meadow which was on Mottingham Farm until the road was driven through in the 1930s.

The grassland is filled with wildflowers in the summer. It is

mostly neutral grassland which hosts corky–fruited water dropwort, fairy flax, wild onion (Allium triquetrum) and rough hawkbit, all of which are less common in Greenwich. On the crest of the hill, on a small patch of acid grassland, are sheep's sorrel and common cat's ear. And common blue and meadow brown butterflies flit among the flowers.

Why 'Harmony' Wood? I don't know!

Many of the trees were planted by children from Horn Park and Middle Park Schools in 1986 and 2002. The path through the woods is very wet and muddy at times, and it can also be very slippery.

At the top of the hill on this long site, King John's Walk connects Eltham with old Mottingham Village, and at the other end, near the Dutch House pub, you find the River Quaggy in a hollow.

The area south of the A20 is less diverse, and closed to the public. Here the Little Quaggy flows alongside the road, "One of the few sections of river with natural banks in Greenwich borough, it supports wetland vegetation including hairy sedge, marsh foxtail, gipsywort, floating sweet–grass and water figwort."[64]

Do walk here on a warm summer's day when the wildflowers are filled with insects — it is really lovely!

Access: Joan Crescent SE9 5RP
Opening times: Always open
Facilities: None; the Green Chain Walk crosses the extreme east of the site
Designation: Nature Reserve,
SINC of Borough Importance Grade 1
Size: 9.74 hectares (24 acres)

Left: *The Quaggy in full flow*
Opposite: *Sidcup Grasslands in summer*

Southwood Park & Southwood Rough

For centuries, Pope Street was a small farming hamlet on crossroads, south east of the Avery Hill Estate. The Pope Street Railway Station opened in 1878 and was renamed New Eltham and Pope Street ten years later. It is said that the station was paid for by the developer, who started building a substantial homes in the area shortly afterwards. More houses appeared after WWI, but the area remained rural well into the 1950s.

The parks were named after Southwood House, where Col J T North lived while his Avery Hill Mansion was rebuilt nearby.

Today, the park is in three parts: a children's play area and outdoor gym alongside the New Eltham Library, a large playing field, and Southwood Rough, a smaller green meadow separated from the playing field by hedging and trees. From 1898, Southwood Rough (the back field) was a cricket field. The playing field next to the library was initially owned by Chiesman's Department Store in Lewisham, and after WWII it was bought by the London Electricity Board. In the late 1970s Greenwich Council bought the ground.

Southwood Park has a new Friends Group which is working hard on improvements. They have planted thousands of snowdrops and crocuses near the playground and created a colourful show in the spring.

The playing field has new trees, and there are plans to extend the paved perimeter path. The grass is managed as both conservation and meadow.

The scrubland and hedgerows around Southwood Rough made this a SINC of Local Importance.

The mix of hawthorn, elder, holly, elm and oak in the hedgerow on the south of the field suggest an old hedge. There was once a small stream hidden in the woodland between the two fields which then turned sharply left at the railway line, but now it is dry. In 1988, elm tree stumps were found here, and the Ecology Report of 1989 tells of Yorkshire fog, dock, red dead nettle and teasel. The report also suggested this might be an educational nature reserve.

Sadly, bramble has taken over, and the borough report of 2017 recommends either considerable remedial work or removal of the SINC designation.

Access: Southwood Road SE9 2AB
Opening times: Always open
Facilities: Playground, outdoor gym
Designation: Southwood Park is a Public Park
Size: Southwood Park 4.5 hectares (11 acres)
Friends of Southwood Park: www.facebook.com

The view from Southwood Rough through to
Southwood Park on a sunny winter's day

The Progress Estate

Cecil Henry Polhill–Turner (1860–1938) inherited real estate and investments from Sir Henry Page–Turner Barron, 2nd Bart, which made him a very wealthy man indeed. The real estate included land in Kidbrooke/Eltham because a past relative was Sir Gregory Page who owned the Wricklemarsh Estate.

In 1903, the Borough of Woolwich bought land from Polhill and his trustees to build a tramway from Woolwich to Eltham along today's Well Hall Road. In January 1915, the government bought another c.95 acres of farmland from the trustees to build the remarkable Well Hall Estate.

At the outbreak of WWI, production at the Royal Arsenal munitions factories in Woolwich increased, and the vastly greater workforce needed accommodation. His Majesty's Office of Works took on the challenge for 1,192 dwellings of which 212 were split into ground– and first–floor flats. The estate was to be completed in six months and Herbert Samuel, President of the Local Government Board, wanted the housing to be a showcase estate.

The Project Manager was Frank Baines, a Principal Architect in HM Office of Works. A team of four with domestic architectural experience surveyed the site on a Saturday and completed the layout over the weekend. Work started about three weeks after the builders had been instructed, on a cost plus basis, because there was no time to invite tenders. The architects worked seven days a week, over 5,000 men were employed on the site, and the estate was completed and ready for occupation within twelve months.

GE Philips' plan was chosen from the team of four, and he believed that the estate should look as though "it had grown and not merely been dropped there."[65] His layout respected the contours of the land and he was undoubtedly influenced by Ebenezer Howard, who wrote *Garden Cities of Tomorrow* in 1902, and Raymond Unwin, one of the pioneers of town planning. Both were concerned about the state of housing available to working class people and wanted living conditions to be less crowded, more hygienic, and also aesthetically pleasing.

The priority was accommodation and so there were no shops, schools or churches in the estate. However, all the houses had generous back gardens, and existing trees were incorporated into the design. Two open spaces were created as recreation areas. At the time the estate was surrounded by open fields, and today, it retains a village atmosphere.

In 1925, the estate was sold to Progress Estates Ltd, a subsidiary of the Royal Arsenal Co–operative Society Ltd., and renamed the Progress Estate. By 1980, two thirds of the homes were owner occupied and the remainder were sold to the Hyde Group. The Greenwich Borough Council bought the greens at the same time.

This is a delightful housing estate, with pretty, cared–for gardens; do take time to walk here.

Lovelace Green SE9 1LF

Richard Lovelace (1618–57) was a soldier and a poet who supported Charles I during the English Civil War. He was imprisoned twice but released when Charles was executed.

Very little is known of him after his release. He was engaged to Lucy Sacheverell, but she believed he died in prison and married another suitor. She features in many of his poems and is generally identified with Althea in his poem *To Althea from Prison* with its much–quoted "Stone walls do not a prison make, Nor iron bars a cage."

Sandby Green SE9 6NJ

Paul Sandby (1730–1809) was a founder member of the Royal Academy in 1769. However, he started work as a draughtsman for the Board of Ordnance, mapping the Scottish highlands for military purposes. In 1768, he was appointed Chief Drawing Master at the Royal Military Academy in Woolwich and stayed there till the end of the century. He is best known for his meticulous and detailed landscape paintings in watercolour and development of aquatints.

Both parks are always open
Friends of the Progress Estate:
www.progressestate.blogspot.com

93a
93b

Lovelace Green

Sandby Green

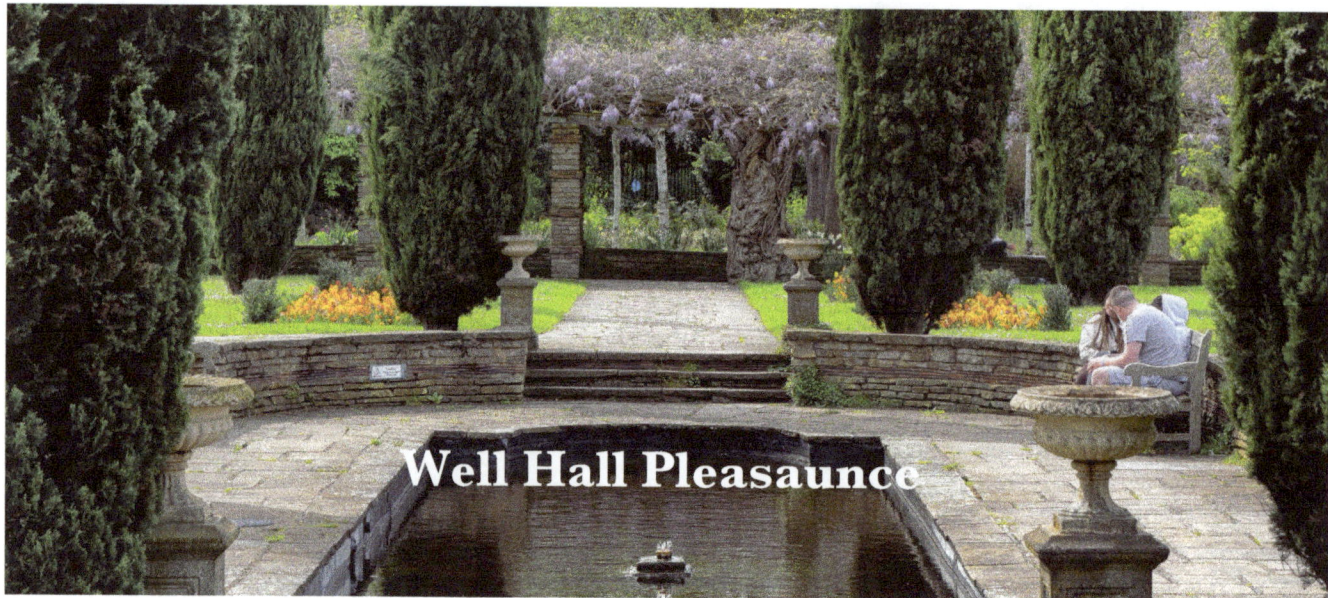

Well Hall Pleasaunce

Sir Jordan de Bricett, who in the 12th century founded the Hospital and Priory of St John of Jerusalem in Clerkenwell, also owned the Manor of Easthorne and the Mansion of Well Hall. The property eventually descended by marriage to the Roper family.

From the mid–16th century, William Roper (1495–1578) and his family owned the estate. His wife Margaret Roper was Sir Thomas More's daughter. Their house stood on today's moat island, and the garden walls and the moat date from that time.

In 1733, the Ropers sold the estate with c.200 hundred acres of farmland to Sir Gregory Page of Wricklemarsh in Blackheath. He replaced the Tudor house with a new house, Well Hall, which lay outside the moat and close to Well Hall Road. From 1899–1922 the tenants were Hubert Bland and Edith Nesbit (*The Railway Children* author).

In 1930, the council bought Well Hall for a park to service the new housing in the area. The house and farm buildings were demolished and J Sutcliffe, Borough Engineer, and his successor H W Tee, laid out differently themed gardens. The park opened in 1933. More land was acquired, and the barn was restored and converted to an art gallery and restaurant which opened in 1936.

The grounds are mostly as originally planned, although the plant nurseries, tennis courts and putting green have gone, and the swannery and peacocks have been replaced by ducks in the moat.

A sunken garden leads into an Italian garden with a long pond and pergola draped with an ancient wisteria, and on to a heather garden with a rockery and another pond. The bowling club enjoys a secluded position in this area. And a little woodland walk hides next to the open meadow beyond the bowling green.

A former coat–of–arms garden and small rockery garden face Well Hall Road, and behind this is the rose garden, formerly the 18th century walled kitchen garden.

The Well Hall stream, a Quaggy tributary, used to flow into the moat, but since 2016, the moat has been topped up with borehole water from the underground aquifer. A stream, fed by piped water, still flows out through the wooded glen.

The Tudor Barn in April

The Friends have produced a useful guide to the many beautiful and mature trees in the park.

This beautiful and elegant little park, created with care by Messrs Sutcliffe and Tee, continues to provide welcome calm and respite from the busy surrounding roads. The Friends won a well deserved Gold Medal in London in Bloom, 2024.

Access: Well Hall Road SE9 6SZ
Opening times: Always open
Facilities: Seats, bowling green, adventure play area, toilets, restaurant, grassed picnic area
Designation: Grade II listed site, Green Flag Public Park, SINC of Local Importance
Size: 4.5 hectares (11 acres)
Friends of Well Hall Pleasaunce: www.wellhall.org.uk

Endnotes

1   Walker, George Alfred, *Gatherings from Graveyards*, (first published 1839, www.babel.hathitrust.org/cgi/pt?id=hvd. hc2jzn&view=1up&seq=25), p.v

2   Tee, H W, *The Provision of Open Spaces*, (July 1937, Journal of The Royal Sanitary Institute, Vol LVIII, no.10)

3   Tudge, Colin, *The Secret Life of Trees*, (2006, Penguin Books), p.8

4   Lysons, Daniel, *The Environs of London*, (first published 1796, Vol.4, www.british-history.ac.uk), pp.359–385

5   Strype, John, *A Survey of the Cities of London and Westminster*, (first published 1603, Book I, Chap.6, online at www. dhi.ac.uk/strype/index.jsp), p.29

6   Besant, Sir Walter, *London South of the Thames*, (first published 1912, reprinted by Forgotten Books) p.208

7   Fields in Trust, www.fieldsintrust.org/News/protect-80-years-on-from-the-first-king-georges-field

8   Daniel Lysons, *The Environs of London*, (first published 1796, Vol.4, https://www.british-history.ac.uk), pp.426–493

9   Sweet, Robert, *The Hothouse and Greenhouse Manual*, (first published 1831, 5th edition, www.pure.uva.nl), pp.205-208

10 Twist, A F, *Widening Circles in Finance, Philanthropy and the Arts; A Study of the life of John Julius Angerstein 1735-1823*, (2002, Thesis externally prepared, University of Amsterdam, www.pure.uva.nl)

11 Hart, F H, *History of Lee and its Neighbourhood*, 1882, (republished by Leopold Classic Library), p.83

12 Ellie Truscott of Knight Dragon, email of 22.9.2023

13 Dr Mills, Mary, *Greenwich Peninsula, Greenwich Marsh — History of an Industrial Heartland*, (2000, Amazon), p.206

14 Lakie, James, www.amazingarchitecture.com

15 Hilary Peters, https://www.theguardian.com/environment/2022/feb/17/hilary-peters-obituary

16 Christchurch School Community Garden, https://www.cscg.info/blank-page-1

17 Burton, John F, *Vertebrate fauna of Blackheath and Greenwich Park*, (2001, London Naturalist No.80), p.49; www.archive.org/stream/londonnaturalist80lond/londonnaturalist80lond_djvu.txt

18 Hasted, Edward, *The History and Topographical Survey of Kent*, (first published 1797, Vol.1, Bristow, Canterbury, 1797), pp.420–441 and https://www.british-history.ac.uk/survey-kent/vol1/

19 Thorne, James, *Handbook to the Environs of London*, (first published 1876, republished by Godfrey Cave Associates 1983), p.50

20 Report commissioned from Social Life, http://www.social-life.co/project/berkeley-group/

21 Haw, George, *From Workhouse to Westminster; The Life Story of Will Crooks M.P.*, (1908, Eld & Blackham), p.246

22 HTA Design, https://issuu.com/landscape-institute/docs/12481_landscape_issue_2-2021_v9_issuu/s/12106345

23 CPRE, *Ten New Parks for London*, https://www.cprelondon.org.uk/news/ten-new-parks-campaign-update/

24 Sarah McMichael, Chairman, Lee Forum

25 "MOL is strategic open land within the urban area. It receives less publicity than Green Belt, but has equal legal status; it is a designation that protects open land within the city, as opposed to around the edge. MOL is specific to London, and can be applied to open space that contributes to the structure of the city, provides open air facilities for sport and recreation, contains features of historic or biodiversity value, and/or forms part of the green infrastructure network." www.gigl.org.uk

26 Hulme, James, *The Industrial Development of Charlton Riverside*, (http://www.glias.org.uk/journals/16-b.pdf)

27 Vincent, W T T, *Records of the Woolwich District*, (first published 1890, Vol.II, republished by FamLoc), p.1022

28 Hasted, Edward, 'Parishes: Charlton', in *The History and Topographical Survey of the County of Kent*, (first published 1797, Vol.I, Canterbury), pp. 420–441, British History Online http://www.british-history.ac.uk/survey-kent/vol1/pp420–441

29 Cecil, The Hon Mrs Evelyn, *London Parks and Gardens*, (1907, Archibald, Constable and Co), p.358ff

30 Besant, Walter, *London South of The Thames*, (first published 1912, republished by Forgotten Books), p.206

31 *Bradshaw's Illustrated Handbook to London*, first published 1862, republished by Conway, 2012), p.182

32   Vincent, W T T, *Records of the Woolwich District,* (first published 1890, Vol I, republished by FamLoc Books, 2015), p.39

33   Thorne, James, *Handbook to the Environs of London,* (first published 1876, republished by Godfrey Cave Associates, 1983), p.740

34   Evening Standard New Homes Awards 2022: https://www.standard.co.uk/homesandproperty/property-news/new-homes-awards-2022-winning-homes-designs-conversions-london-commuter-b1030220.html

35   Berkeley Homes, Maribor Park, https://docs.planning.org.uk/20240319/53/_GRNW_DCAPR_119429/wp8cj7hsoja08gp8.pdf

36   Newsome et al, English Heritage Report, (https://historicengland.org.uk/research/results/reports/14-2009), p.7

37   *Survey of London, Vol.48, Woolwich,* (2012, Yale University Press, Andrew Saint, General Editor), p.48

38   Holmes, Isabella, *London Burial Grounds,* (first published 1896, British Library Historical Print Edition), p.240

39   https://en.wikipedia.org/wiki/Tom_Cribb

40   *Living in the Landscape,* LDA Design for Peabody, p.3

41   Peabody Trust, *Living in the Landscape,* www.thamesmeadnow.org.uk/the-plan/thamesmeads-landscapes/

42   Thorne, James, *Handbook to the Environs of London,* (first published 1896, republished 1983, Godfrey Cave Associates), p.472

43   Sexby, Lt Col J J, *The Municipal Parks, Gardens, and Open Spaces of London: their History and Associations,* (first published 1905, republished by Scholar Select), p.50

44   Mogridge, George, *Old Humphrey's Walks in London and its Neighbourhood, (1799,* The Religious Tract Society), p.314

45   Plumstead Cemetery, www.thelondondead.blogspot.com/

46   Plumstead Cemetery, www.thelondondead.blogspot.com/

47   The Victoria Cross, www.cwgc.org

48   Vincent, W T T, *Records of the Woolwich District,* (first published 1890, Vol II, republished by FamLoc Books), p.775

49   Holmes, Mrs Isabella, *The London Burial-Grounds,* (first published 1896, British Library Historical Reprint), pp. 90 & 103

50   Holmes, Mrs Isabella, *The London Burial Grounds,* (first published 1896, British Library Historical Reprint), p.100

51   Laurence Binyon, http://www.greatwar.co.uk/poems/laurence-binyon-for-the-fallen.htm

52   Hasted, Edward, *The History and Topographical Survey of the County of Kent,* (first published 1797, Vol.I, www.british-history.ac.uk/survey-kent/vol1/, pp.455-491)

53   Besant, Sir Walter, *London South of the Thames,* (first published 1912, reprinted by Forgotten Books), p.319
https://www.jstor.org/stable/40102030

54   Jerry Coleby-Williams, https://jerry-coleby-williams.net/2021/03/16/avery-hill-mansion-and-winter-garden-recollections-of-a-fading-part-of-londons-horticultural-heritage/

55   Cecil, The Hon Mrs Evelyn, *London Parks and Gardens,* (1907, Archibald Constable & Co Ltd, London), p.183

56   Butts, Robert, *Butts' Historical Guide to Lewisham, Ladywell, Lee, Blackheath and Eltham,* (first published 1878, digitised by the British Library, printed by Amazon), p.38

57   Butts, Robert, *Butts' Historical Guide to Lewisham, Ladywell, Lee, Blackheath and Eltham,* (first published 1878, digitised by the British Library, printed by Amazon), p.37

58   Butts, Robert, *Butts' Historical Guide to Lewisham, Ladywell, Lee, Blackheath and Eltham,* (first published 1878, digitised by the British Library, printed by Amazon), p.38

59   The Eltham Heights Estate, www.londonandkent.co.uk/about-us/eltham-heights-1935/

60   Jean Froissart, *Chronicles,* p.168, https://archive.org/stream/chroniclesoffroi00froi/chroniclesoffroi00froi_djvu.txt

61   Cherry, B and Pevsner, N, *The Buildings of England, London 2: South,* (1983; Yale University Press, 2002), p.302

62   Evelyn, John, *Diary, 1620-1706,* (1908, Macmillan & Co), p.231

63   Holmes, Mrs Isabella, *The London Burial-Grounds,* (first published 1896, British Library Historical Reprint), p.103

64   www.gigl.org.uk/sinc/GrBl10/

65   Beaufoy, S L G, *Well Hall Estate, Eltham: An example of good housing built in 1915,* (The Town Planning Review, vol.21, no.3, October 1950, pp.259-271, www.jstor.org/stable/40102030)

ALPHABETICAL LIST OF GREEN SPACES

Books and written Sources

Ackroyd, Peter, *Thames: Sacred River,* (2007, Chatto & Windus)

Aslet, Clive, *The Story of Greenwich,* (1999, Fourth Estate, London)

Baedeker, Karl, *London and its Environs, 1881,* (2013, reprinted Isha Books)

Bagnold, Colonel A H, Extracts from *The Parish Magazine, Christ Church, Shooters Hill,* September 1936–August 1938, Greenwich Archive

Barker, Felix, *Greenwich and Blackheath Past,* (1999, Historical Publications)

Beaufoy, S L G, *Well Hall Estate, Eltham: An Example of Good Housing Built in 1915,* (October 1950, The Town Planning Review, vol.21, no.3), pp.259–271; www.jstor.org/stable/40102030

Besant, Sir Walter, *London South of the Thames, 1912,* (reprinted by Forgotten Books)

Billinghurst, Keith, *The Origins and Evolution of the Progress Estate,* (2017, Brown Dog Books)

Bradshaw's Illustrated Hand Book to London, 1862, (2012, republished by Conway)

Brook, Roy, *The Story of Eltham Palace,* (1960, George G Harrap & Co Ltd)

Bunney, John, Eltham Lodge: *Where Perfection meets Convenience,* (2021, Impress)

Butts, Robert, *Butts' Historical Guide to Lewisham, Ladywell, Lee, Blackheath and Eltham, 1878,* (reprinted by Amazon)

Cecil, The Hon Mrs Evelyn, *London Parks and Gardens,* (1907, Archibalc Constable & Co Ltd)

Chadwick, Peter, and Weaver, Ben, *The Town of Tomorrow: 50 Years of Thamesmead,* (2019, Here Press)

Dews, Nathan, *History of Deptford, 1884,* (2015, republished by FamLoc Books, Michael Wood, (Editor))

Domesday Book, (1992, reprinted Penguin Books)

Drury FSA, Paul, et al, *Visualising Hugh May's Eltham Lodge,* (2019, Antiquaries Journal 99)

Driver, Christopher, (Editor), *John Evelyn Cook,* (1997, Prospect Books)

Egan, Michael, *Kidbrooke, Eight Hundred Years of a Farming Community,* (1983, Greenwich and Lewisham Antiquarian Society)

Egan, Michael, *Wricklemarsh Revisited,* (2017, Kent Archaeological Society, www.kentarchaeology.org.uk)

Elliston–Erwood, F C, *Well Hall,* (1947[3], Metropolitan Borough of Woolwich)

English Heritage, *Eltham Palace,* (2012, English Heritage Guidebooks)

Evelyn, John, *Diary, 1620-1706,* (online at www.gutenberg.org)

Godley, Robert and Celia, *Greenwich; A History of Greenwich, Blackheath, Charlton, Deptford and Woolwich,* (1999, self–published)

Gregory, Richard Robert Castell, *The Story of Royal Eltham, 1909,* (2017, republished FamLoc, Michael Wood, (Editor))

Hart, F H, *A History of Lee and its Neighbourhood, 1882,* (republished by Leopold Classic Library)

Hasted, Edward, *The History and Topographical Survey of the County of Kent, Volume 1, 1797,* (www.british-history.ac.uk/survey-kent/vol1/pp.455–491)

Haw, George, *From Workhouse to Westminster: The Life Story of Will Crooks M.P.,* (1908, Eld & Blackham)

Hawkins, Chris, *The Complete Guide to Greenwich Park,* (2021, Ormidea Publishing)

Lesnes Abbey, (2019, Ormidea Publishing)

Holmes,Isabella M, *The London Burial Grounds, 1896,* (reprinted by The British Library)

Hounsell, Peter, *Bricks of Victorian London,* (2022, University of Hertfordshire Press)

Howard, Ebenezer, *Tomorrow: A Peaceful Path to Real Reform, 1898,* (republished by Cambridge University Press)

Hulme, James, *The Industrial Development of Charlton Riverside,* 2016, (http://www.glias.org.uk/journals/16-b.pdf)

Jefferson, E F E, *The Woolwich Story,* (1970, printed by Instance Printers, Woolwich)

Jenkinson, Sally, *Charlton House, The Story of a Jacobean Mansion,* (1983, Gordon Teachers Centre)

Jennings, Sally, *Georgian Gardens,* (2005, English Heritage)

Kennett, John, *Eltham, A Pictorial History,* (1995, Phillimore and Co Ltd)

LDA Design, *Living in the Landscape,* (2019, commissioned by Peabody)

London Ecology Unit, *Woolwich Common Management Brief,* 1998, (https://friendsofwoolwichcommon.org.uk)

Loudon, John Claudius, *Breathing Spaces for the Metropolis, 1829,* (www.landscapearchitecture.org.uk)

Marshall, Geoff, *London's Docklands, An Illustrated History,* (2018, The History Press)

Mayer, Laura, *Capability Brown and the English Landscape Garden,* (2011, Shire Publications)

Meller, Hugh & Parsons, Brian, *London Cemeteries: An Illustrated Guide and Gazetteer,* (2011[5], The History Press)

Mills, Dr Mary, *Greenwich Marsh – The 300 years before the Dome,* (1999, printed by Biddles Ltd)

The Greenwich Riverside: Upper Watergate to Angerstein, (2021, Amazon)

Greenwich and Woolwich at Work, (2002, Sutton Publishing)

The Industries of Deptford Creek, (no date, printed by Amazon)

Greenwich Peninsula, Greenwich Marsh: History of an Industrial Heartland, (no date, printed by Amazon)

Mogridge, George, *Old Humphrey's Observations,* (1939, The Religous Tract Society)

Old Humphrey's Walks in London, (1843, The Religious Tract Society)

Morris, John K, *Woodland Archaeology in London,* (https://historicengland.org.uk/content/docs/planning/woodland-archaeology-london-pdf/)

Newsome, S and Williams, A, *Woolwich Common: An Assessment of the Historic Environment of Woolwich Common and its Environs,* Historic England, Research Department Report Series no.098-2009, ISSN 1749-8775

Newsome, S, Millward, J, Cocroft, W, *Repository Woods, Woolwich, Greater London; An Archaeological Survey of the Royal Military Repository Training Grounds,* Research Department Report Series 14-2009, English Heritage

Parker, Franklin, *George Peabody: A Biography,* (1995, Vanderbilt University Press)

Pevsner, N and Cherry, B, *The Buildings of England: London 2 – South,* (2002, Yale University Press)

Platts, Beryl, *A History of Greenwich,* (1973[2,] David and Charles Ltd)

Plumstead Common Environment Group, *Our Common Story,* (2004, Prometheus Press)

Powley, Terry, *Eltham Park South: A Short History,* (2012, available from the author)

Priestley, John, *Eltham Palace,* (2013, The History Press)

Quest–Ritson, Charles, *The English Garden: A Social History,* (2001, Penguin Books)

Ramzan, David, *Maritime Greenwich,* (2009, The History Press)

Rhind, Neil, *Blackheath Village and Environs, Vol I, II and III,* (1983, Blackheath Bookshop Limited)

Rhind, Neil and Marshall, Roger, *Walking the Heath,* (2021, The Blackheath Society)

Rhind, Neil and Watson, Julian, *Greenwich Revealed,* (2013, The Blackheath Society)

Saint, Andrew (General Editor): *Survey of London, Vol.48, Woolwich,* (2012, Yale University Press, Peter Guillery, Editor, and online at https://www.ucl.ac.uk/bartlett/architecture/research/survey-london/woolwich)

Sexby, Lt Col J J, *The Municipal Parks, Gardens, and Open Spaces of London; Their History and Associations, 1905,* (Republished by Scholar Select)

Smith, John G, *Charlton: A Compilation of the Parish and its People, Vols.I, II, & III,* (1970, 1975, 1986, privately printed)

Social Life, *Living at Kidbrooke,* (www.social-life.co/media/files/Living_at_Kidbrooke_Village)

Spurgeon, Darrell:

    Discover Greenwich and Charlton, (1991, Greenwich Guide-Books)

    Discover Eltham and its Environs, (1992, Greenwich Guide-Books)

    Discover Woolwich and its Environs, (1996, Greenwich Guide-Books)

    Discover Deptford and Lewisham, (1997, Greenwich Guide-Books)

Steele, Jess, *Turning the Tide: The History of Everyday Deptford,* (1993, Deptford Forum Publishing Ltd)

Stone, Peter: *The History of the Port of London,* (2017, Pen and Sword)

Strong, Roy, *The Renaissance Garden in England,* (1984, Thames and Hudson)

Swales, S, Games, M and Yarham, I, *Nature Conservation in Greenwich,* (1989, London Ecology Unit vol.10)

Symes Michael, *The English Landscape Garden,* (2019, Historic England)

The Eltham Society, *Looking into Eltham,* (1980)

Thorne, James, *Handbook to the Environs of London*, (first published 1876, republished by Godfrey Cave Associate, 1983)

Transport for London: *SuDS in London – a guide*, (November 2016, published by the Mayor of London; https://content.tfl.gov.uk/sustainable-urban-drainage-november-2016.pdf)

Unwin, Sir Raymond, *Nothing gained by overcrowding, 1912*, (republished by Cornell University Library, printed by Amazon)

Van der Merwe, Pieter, *Royal Greenwich: A History in Kings and Queens*, (2020, National Maritime Museum)

Vickers, Denis J, *Woolwich Common: Ecological Survey and Management Plan*, April 2022–March 2027, (https://friendsofwoolwichcommon.org.uk)

Vincent, W T T, *Records of the Woolwich District, Vols 1 & II, 1890*, (republished by FamLoc Books, Michael Wood, Editor)

Wagg, Christine and McHugh, James, *Homes for London: The Peabody Story*, (2017, Peabody)

Walford, Edward, *Village London, Part 3 – South East and South, 1883-84*, (1985, republished by The Alderman Press)

Old and New London, Vol.6, 1878, (online at https://www.british-history.ac.uk/old-new-london/vol6/pp206-223)

Wareham, Tom, *Oxleas*, (2020, printed by Amazon)

Watson, Julian, *St Peter's Abbey, Ghent*; Journal of the Greenwich Historical Society, Vol.3, No.6, 2009

Watson, Julian & Gregory, Kit: *In the Meantime*, (1988, London Borough of Greenwich Tourism Section), (https://www.academia.edu/42468617/St_Peters_Abbey_Ghent)

Way, Twigs, *The Tudor Garden*, (2013, Shire Publications)

Weightman, Colin, *Plumstead Stories*, (www.plumstead-stories.com)

White, Ken, *The Quaggy River and its Catchment Area*, (1999, QWAG)

Wohlleben, Peter,
   The Hidden Life of Trees, (2017, William Collins)
   The Heartbeat of Trees, (2022, William Collins)

Woods, Roberta, *The Chemical Conquistador: Colonel North & His Nitrate Dream House*, (2020, printed by Amazon)

Websites

British Library images, https://imagesonline.bl.uk

British Listed Buildings, https://britishlistedbuildings.co.uk

Caring for God's Acre, https://burialgrounds-places.nbnatlas.org/places/10031962

Cemeteries in London, https://thelondondead.blogspot.com

Charlton Parks Reminiscence Project, https://charltonchampion.files.wordpress.com/2013/01/cprp-booklet.pdf

Edith's Streets, http://edithsstreets.blogspot.com

Find a Grave, https://www.findagrave.com/cemetery/2142512/plumstead-cemetery

Forces War Records, https://www.forces-war-records.co.uk/account/loggedout/?LibSearchCount=0&NameSearchCount=1&AutoRenew=True&RecieveEmails=False&FullMember=True

GiGL, https://www.gigl.org.uk/about-gigl/

Greenwich Borough Council, https://www.royalgreenwich.gov.uk

Greenwich Industrial History, www.greenwichindustrialhistory.blogspot.com

Greenwich Peninsula History, https://greenwichpeninsulahistory.wordpress.com/links-and-resources/

Greenwich Wildlife Network, www.greenwichwildlifenetwork.org/blog

Hathi Trust Digital Library, https://www.hathitrust.org

Heritage Gateway, www.heritagegateway.org.uk

Historic England, www.historicengland.org.uk

Ideal Homes — a history of south east London suburbs, www.ideal-homes.org.uk

Kent Underground Research Group, https://kurg.org.uk/chalk-mines

Key to English place names, http://kepn.nottingham.ac.uk

Landscape Architecture in London, https://www.gardenvisit.com
London Geodiversity Partnership, www.londongeopartnership.org.uk
London Metropolitan Archives, www.search.lma.gov.uk/
London Parks and Gardens, www.londongardenstrust.org
Lost Hospital and Almshouses of London, www.ezitis.myzen.co.uk
Maps online:
- Ordnance Survey Maps online, www.nls.co.uk
- MAPCO, www.mapco.net
- Old Maps Online, www.oldmapsonline.org
- The British Geological Survey: https://www.bgs.ac.uk
- John Rocque Map of London, 1761: https://geo.southwark.gov.uk/connect/analyst/Includes/Historical%20map%20scans/200dpi/John%20Rocques%20A%20Plan%20of%20London%201766.pdf
Mary Evans Picture Library, www.prints-online.com/galleries/
Open Spaces Society, www.oss.org.uk
Plumstead Particular, www.plumsteadparticular.uk
Plumstead Stories, www.plumstead-stories.com
Royal Arsenal History, www.royal-arsenal-history.com
SENine archive, (online at www.senine.co.uk) The Corbett Society, www.thecorbettsociety.org.uk
The Royal Observatory Greenwich, www.royalobservatorygreenwich.org
The Underground Map, www.theundergroundmap.com
Trees in burial grounds, www.burialgrounds-places.nbnatlas.org

www.ingramcontent.com/pod-product-compliance
Lightning Source LLC
Chambersburg PA
CBHW041802280326
41926CB00104B/4773